The Best of Both Worlds

Also by Gordon Smith:

One Hundred Answers from Spirit

GORDON SMITH

The Best of Both Worlds

CORONET

First published in Great Britain in 2014 by Coronet
An imprint of Hodder & Stoughton
An Hachette UK company

First published in paperback in 2016

1

Copyright © Gordon Smith 2014

The right of Gordon Smith to be identified as the Author
of the Work has been asserted by him in accordance with the
Copyright, Designs and Patents Act 1988.

A CIP catalogue record for this title is available from the British Library

Paperback ISBN: 978 1 444 79082 5
Ebook ISBN: 978 1 444 79085 6

Typeset in Plantin Light by Palimpsest Book Production Limited,
Falkirk, Stirlingshire

Printed and bound by CPI Group (UK) Ltd, Croydon, CRO 4YY

Hodder & Stoughton policy is to use papers that are natural, renewable
and recyclable products and made from wood grown in sustainable
forests. The logging and manufacturing processes are expected to
conform to the environmental regulations of the country of origin.

Hodder & Stoughton Ltd
Carmelite House
50 Victoria Embankment
London EC4Y 0DZ

www.hodder.co.uk

To my parents, 'Lizzie and Sammy'.
Gorbals die-hards, who because of this book
will never really die.
With love and thanks from all the family.

Prologue

Nothing drags your thinking into the past like a death in the family. It's one of those things that will make you look for an understanding of who you are and where you are going in your own life. Yes, death definitely makes us look for answers. That's exactly what I was doing when I heard a loud announcement directly above my head that made me jolt forward in my seat. 'Cabin Crew seats for take-off.'

The next day was to be my mother's funeral. I had been working at a spiritual congress in Switzerland when she passed. This had left me with a terrible sense of helplessness and separation from someone who had always been so present in my life.

In the past four days since my sister Joan called to tell me that Mother had gone I think I had re-lived many episodes in my memory that featured this very special yet sometimes very difficult woman. She was a big influence on not just me, but on all of her children. I had been at a seminar full of people who were talking about life after death and the survival of the human spirit. I was supposed to be there to provide them with all the answers, which I did to the best of my ability, but now I just wanted to think about my mother.

The drinks had just been served and the stranger next to me made no attempt to make conversation, staring deep into his gin and tonic, much like a crystal gazer, I thought, before returning to my memories. My mother's personality was so potent it seemed that anyone who met her felt the urge to impersonate her. She was always so animated and infectious. Lizzy (as she was known to all her family) was always larger than life. She was easy to make laugh and just as easy to upset. I am sure all of us in the family would agree that you'd never refer to our mother as ordinary, in between or contented; she was either up or down, black or white. There was never much middle with Lizzy.

I must have gone through the full spectrum of human emotions on that short flight from Zurich to London. I laughed out loud when I recalled my mother walking into the salon I had worked in back in Glasgow some twenty odd years earlier. Her face was bursting with rage as she ripped off her headscarf to reveal a mass of bright green frizzy hair. Right in that moment it clashed with the high, angry red tone moving through her cheeks and the white scarf which had dropped onto her shoulders. She resembled a deranged version of the Italian flag.

My mother often mucked around with hair dye, so this wasn't the first time I had had to deal with this type of situation. She had been brought up in poor times which left her always looking for a bargain. She loved to rummage through the cheap bins in stores, only this time she must have bought a tint that was well out of date. As bizarre as this scene was I knew not to laugh in my mother's face. No, Lizzy had a vile temper and in such situations all of my family and friends knew not to provoke that volcanic side of mommy dearest.

'Look at the state of my fucking hair. What do you think

happened?' she demanded. Her bright green eyes seemed somehow more prominent than ever. (Did I mention that Lizzy swears a lot?)

This is a comb mother, not a magic wand! was how I wanted to answer, waving my comb in front of her. But the natural tact of the hairdresser prevailed and I jumped into hairdresser shock-mask-mode as I told her instead how unfortunate she was to have got a bad tint but how easy it was to put right.

I wonder what she would have thought if she'd known what was running through my mind at the time – and, I'm sure, the minds of the rest of the staff; all the witty things that could have been said in that moment, including references to lawnmowers, or hedge cutters and Crusty the Clown from *The Simpsons*. I even saw the image of a goat standing behind her, munching away on her leafy-looking hair. My body became so racked with quiet laughter that I really had to fight hard to control myself.

I could sense that the man sitting next to me was looking my way. He was probably wondering what this crazy guy beside him was laughing about. Rather than try to explain, I did one of those things people do when caught laughing to themselves in a public place. I coughed and rubbed my nose whilst sniffing a lot, like I had hay fever. I think I waved my hand a few times in front of my face and gave a pathetic look in the man's direction before drifting back into thoughts of my green-haired mother.

It was as if I was opening a drawer in a familiar old dressing table, looking for something I knew was in there, as I pulled my thoughts around in search of memories of the softer side of my mother. I couldn't find any, but I remembered how sad I would feel for her as she told us stories about her upbringing in the Gorbals, a pretty poor place to grow up in during the 1920s, 30s and 40s. There were many stories she had told me and my brothers when we were just young boys about how at Christmas she would wait with her younger brothers and sisters for their mother to come home from her day selling secondhand clothes at the old flea-market on Christmas Eve to see if she had a Christmas present for them. If they were lucky they would find an orange or a banana inside a sock, bulked up with ashes. I'll never forget how my heart used to drop with sympathy at hearing this, how I would choke back tears. Sammy and John, who were older than me, would start to laugh and tease her. Lizzy would laugh along with them and tell them that it was the normal thing for people of her time and from that poor place, but I always felt that there was a deep sadness in her as she told us this. I think it was the ashes. They made me think of empty wishes in some way.

Now her toughness in the face of the things she had to contend with made me want to cry for her, maybe because she had never been able to cry for herself. To be sad showed weakness in Lizzy's eyes. She had learned to laugh at her hardships and make offhand, witty comments that gave her some sort of control over her past. The truth is that my brothers and sisters and I had very privileged lives because of what she gave us, and maybe that was what she was trying to get through to us when she told us her stories.

The man next to me was staring at me again. I didn't really care now as I wiped away tears from my face. I thought about what Lizzy might say. It would probably begin with, 'What the fuck are you looking at?' I sought distraction in the in-flight magazine which, it turned out, was a better screen than source of reading material.

Seat-belt lights came on above our heads as the plane was beginning to descend into London. I remember feeling that I was getting nearer to home. The humming and whistling of the big engines brought us gently back down to earth. I still had to catch a connecting flight on to Glasgow before I would feel that I was truly close to my mother's spirit. I don't know why I felt this but I did. For most of my adult life I had been telling people that the spirits of those we love are close to us and that they are with us everywhere we go and, though I did and do believe that to be so, I hadn't felt that my mother's spirit had been close to me since her passing.

The connecting flight was bang on time. This would have pleased Lizzy. Before I knew it I was in my seat again, buckled up with my armrest down and seat-back up in preparation for the next take-off.

I noticed it was getting dark outside as we shot up into the misty, grey night sky over London. As the aeroplane moved forward my memories ran backwards and I knew why. I wanted to scour my mind for every last precious memory of my mother's life. I wanted to find the funny ones and the sad ones and most of all, I wanted to find the ones that defined Lizzy and made her the woman that everyone knew.

I had been asked to speak about her life at the funeral service and I wanted it to be special, because for all her faults, she really meant the world to all of us. I wanted to re-create some of the events of her life and animate them in such an authentic way that we could all feel that we had her there with us for one more moment. In the end, I wanted to do her justice and remind everyone of the important strengths and qualities she had displayed and hopefully passed on to us during her eighty-six years in this world.

As I settled into the flight I began to think about how strong Lizzy was physically and mentally throughout her life. I knew this would be something I would concentrate on in my talk. Memories began to run through my mind like little streams and I knew that something was trying to reveal itself to me. All of a sudden I was seeing myself as a small boy. I was about three years old and I was holding my mother's hand as she walked with me by her side and I remember I was looking up at her and talking. I knew for certain I was talking because my mother always said that from the moment I learned to talk, I never shut my mouth. Thanks Lizzy.

As my mother and I continued to walk, we came to a familiar sight, the house we lived in then and through much of my childhood, 97 Mansel Street in Balornock. We'd moved there when I was two, into a block of four apartments in a big, black house. It was on the north side of Glasgow, and we'd moved there because dad wanted a garden. It's strange how long the path up to the front door seemed to be in my memory, yet I know that it was really only about five metres long.

Then, out of nowhere came a horrible memory, something I knew I had experienced but for some reason unknown to me must have been kept hidden away deep inside of me in some distant department of my mind. I was standing on this black, tar-covered garden path when I felt a surge run through my body. I now know it was the first time I had experienced this emotion. It was fear. And now I could see why I was so scared. My mother had suddenly let go of my hand. Looking back at myself as a small boy I realized that the child I was watching must have sensed that there was a fear in his mother, perhaps by the abrupt way she relinquished her grasp. I felt the child's fear deeply.

Lizzy was now walking slowly into our empty house calling out loudly, 'Who's in here? I know somebody's in here.' As I looked back at the memory it was as if I could feel the adrenalin running through my mother's body. She continued slowly along the narrow hall. A force field of nervous strength had erected around her that seemed to pulse and as a small boy I felt connected to the rhythm of that pulse. Then my mother disappeared into one of the three bedrooms that connected to the entrance hall. In that moment a new level of fear rose in the child as his mother disappeared from sight. The strange thing was I could somehow distinguish both the child's fear and how it differed from his mother's. Both were connected yet individual. The whole thing reminded me of a lioness sensing danger close and preparing to stand in front of her cub no matter what lay in wait.

My mother knew that there was someone in our flat that day. She knew because as we had walked down the path that morning returning from the local shops she had noticed that the front door was ajar. Who knows what was going through her mind as she walked into this unknown and potentially very dangerous situation? Many people would have run or called out for help, but my mother wasn't like other people, especially when it came to her home or her children.

The intense silence that had built up was broken by a deafening roar. It was a roar that I would hear many times in my life after this, 'Ahhrrrrrrrrrrrr!' The hunt was over and the loud yell was my mother. She had caught a man hiding under one of the beds. I would later learn that he had broken into our house to steal clothes from my eldest brother Tommy's wardrobe and had been disturbed by us coming back up the path. He hadn't had time to think. He had been just about to leave by the front door when he'd heard my chatter and shot under the nearest bed, probably hoping to escape once we had settled into the living room.

From the child's view, all I could see now was one body standing, bent over another which was crawling and clambering around the floor of our hall, being punched, kicked and battered like an old cod.

'You bastard, I'll fucking kill you, you dirty little thieving bastard.'

'Please, Mrs Smith, please let me go, I'm sorry.' The young man rolled out of our front door doubled over and staggered to his feet holding his stomach with one hand while with the other was still trying to protect his face as he tried to edge past where I was standing.

'Sorry are yae? You'll be even mer sorry when oor Tommy gets home ya fucking cowardly thief.' It was one of our neighbours and he knew that what my mother did to him was nothing compared to what my brother would do to him later. It was a different time back then and a different generation that dealt with things in a different way.

'Strength and courage,' I whispered to no one as I remembered how quickly Lizzy picked up the bag of shopping from the path once she'd seen the burglar off. She had let it down beside me before going in to tackle him. Then she looked down at me like I was another bag of shopping she had set down. 'Come on, move you and get in here I've no got all fucking day.' I felt filled with energy both in the present and as a child in the memory; a real rousing feeling in my gut, there was something about knowing that you were being protected by this type of strong person. At three years old a person doesn't know right or wrong but they do know when they are being protected. This was my mother demonstrating her love.

The plane was getting closer to the earth now and I was relieved that I had a theme to build my talk on. I could just see the lights of Glasgow below me coming into view, a great orange mass and knew I was close when we hit the first bump of turbulence in the air above my home city. I'm sure there is a hole in the sky above Glasgow because even on a clear night the plane always bumps above the Campsie Hills on the approach to the airport. The bump jolted my thinking and I became aware that for the first time in my life I was going to be in Glasgow when Lizzy wouldn't be there physically. Bang, clatter, bump. More bumps on the way to landing. They felt just like my mother's slaps, slaps to tell me not to think like that. She could be so tough at times yet reassuring when you needed her to be.

So many thoughts, memories and reflections were bubbling to the surface as we landed. I was four years old and with Lizzy in the centre of Glasgow on a busy Saturday afternoon. It was one of my earliest memories and emotionally charged. As usual, I was holding tight to my mother's hand as she always instructed. I clearly recall looking around me at all the people in the busy street. It filled me with excitement and wonder. Then, for some reason, I let go of my mother's hand. There was a second or two when I felt that everything was still in a street heaving with people passing by in all directions, too much for a four-year-old to take in. Then I *realized* that I had let go of my mother's hand and that I was on my own. Again that same memory of fear filled me at the thought of losing my mother and for the second time in the four days since I'd been told that she had died I felt as helpless as that little four-year-old boy in my memory.

I remember how I'd screamed with pure alarm, 'Mammy, mammy, mammy, mammy, mammy!' I felt this moment of sheer panic like it was yesterday. In the middle of a hectic Argyll Street, passers-by stopped and reacted. 'Has somebody lost a wee boy?' somebody was shouting over the heads of the crowd and in no time Lizzy was there yelling and swearing. Then she crouched down in front of me, holding both my arms, probably just as relieved as I was and said to me, 'It's ok I've got you now, son.' I was safe. It was the strangest thing because at that moment the plane touched down in Glasgow and I felt that same sense of relief to be back with my mother again. It didn't matter that I was fifty years old or that I now have an understanding of life after death. As I heard the voice of the purser say, 'Ladies and gentlemen, welcome to Glasgow!' I truly felt like that little four-year-old being safely gathered up by his mother.

I

Mother, Music And Mayhem

It was the summer of 1966 and I was four years old. It was a very hot day, all the windows in the house were open and the street outside was full of the sounds of children playing. A group of boys was kicking an old burst leather football from one pavement to the other while a dog chased the old, airless object from one side of the street to the other, barking constantly in its frustration.

Girls further along the pavement were playing with skipping ropes and singing little songs as they jumped in and out of the ropes. '*On the mountain stands a castle and the owner Frankenstein with his daughter Pansy Potter she my only valentine.*' From where I was standing looking out of our living room window I could see much of what was happening in our street and the noise coming from all different directions just seemed to be full of vitality and joy. It all seemed to be saying one thing and to me that was 'LIFE'.

I believe I have a strong memory, but most of my memories as a four-year-old are bitty to say the least. Yet for some bizarre reason this moment stands out very clearly in my mind. In one room The Beatles were belting out the latest number one hit as my eldest brother Tommy was getting dressed to go out, humming loudly. From somewhere else I could hear the sounds of Diana Ross and the Supremes competing with the Fab Four as my sister Betty tried to keep up and sing along. Yet somehow my mother could top all the noise as she called out, 'Sammy, make them turn that fucking music aff, ah canny hear myself think in here!'

It must have been a Sunday because it was the only time of the week that both my parents seemed to be in our kitchen at the same time. I don't remember my father being in my life much when I was that young. Not because he was an absent dad, no, but because he was always working all the hours God sent, usually doing some kind of heavy manual labour. Sunday was a day when he liked to be with the family, often helping Lizzy prepare Sunday lunch or playing with some of us in the house or in the garden and we were all happier for that. 'Lizzy, for God's sake, they're only young, let them play their music.' It all depended on my mother's mood how she would respond. If she was agitated she might say, 'My nerves are up to high fucking doh, so shut that rubbish up.'

My mother complained about her nerves all through my childhood. She swore like a trooper, but there were certain words that never crossed her lips. Anything relating to sexual parts or women's problems could never be spoken about. On the other hand, if Lizzy was happy she would sometimes just smile at my dad, shake her head and give a loud sigh. On occasion she'd even try to sing along with the words if she liked the song – my mother, like Betty was a very good singer. On this particular day she sang and it was one of the very happiest memories from my early childhood, all the family being together and harmony in the air all around me.

I count this memory as my first ever sense of being happy in this world. It stands out amongst memories of much harsher emotional experiences. Fear and rage certainly always come to my mind more readily than joy when I look back over my young life. I didn't know it then, but I was a sensitive child. I don't mean I was wimpy or squeamish, but I was very sensitive to the atmosphere around me.

I had just turned four in the summer of 1966 and I was the youngest of seven children. Tommy, Betty, Joan, Agnes, Sammy, Jonny and finally me. After several months of unsuccessful treatment for a stomach ailment, Agnes had died aged nearly two some years before I was born. All the rest of us were crammed into the house in the north of Glasgow. If that wasn't enough people, my cousin Sandra who was around eighteen or nineteen when I was four was living with us as well. All that energy could create a force for joy when it was harmonious and flowing, but it could become quite explosive when personalities began to collide.

Another of my earliest memories comes from when I was around six years old. Sandra was becoming increasingly annoyed at the way Sammy, who would have been ten, was eating his dinner. He could be an annoying boy. He loved to shock people, especially the older members of the family. On this occasion he was slurping his food deliberately because he knew it would really upset her, while pretending to be unaware whenever she told him to stop it. Of course this added further to her frustration.

'Sammy, that's turnin' ma fuckin' stomach!'

'A'm nae doin' anything!'

'I swear to God I'll kick yer fuckin' head in!'

Maybe this kind of thing happens in all big families, but I suppose what followed wasn't so usual. This was our evening meal when we all sat where we could around the living room, balancing plates of food on our laps, usually watching TV – *Crossroads* or whatever happened to be on. I can remember the feeling in my stomach getting tighter to the point that I couldn't eat anymore. My mother came in from the kitchen where she had just prepared all the food for everyone. My mother had a typical, pale Irish complexion that flushed with anger easily. Now she was bright red and breathing fast. She began to shout at me, 'Eat that fuckin' dinner, that's what you asked for.' I was a fussy eater then – I wouldn't eat vegetables – and needed something different to eat from the rest of the family. On that day I think it was fish boiled in milk.

But now, my lack of appetite was being caused by the tension. I could tell that something bad was about to happen any second. I knew the back and forward jibes between my brother and his older cousin were going to be enough to ignite my mother's very short fuse. It felt as though the atmosphere in the room was getting tighter and tighter with each comment.

'Sammy,' Sandra said. 'You better stop that! I'm warning you, if you dae that wan mer time I'll punch yae, ya wee shite.' I remember that when Sandra got angry her eyes would bulge and it made her quite scary-looking. But Sammy was never one to back down in the face of another person's aggression, and he carried on with his little act, looking up towards my mother with the most innocent of expressions. 'Ma, I don't know what she means, I'm no daen anything I swear, she's imagining things – she's mental.'

It continued like this until Lizzy could take no more of it, and the explosion happened.

'Bastards, the fucking lot awe yae.' Smash! A plate full of food hit the wall above where my brother was sitting. Mother had hurled her own plate in the general direction of Sammy and Sandra, not really caring which one she hit. Before any protests could be made she had her hand around Sandra's throat while the other was slapping out in Sammy's direction. Joan, Betty and Jonny had managed to squirm sideways out into the hall, but I was riveted to my chair. By now food was on the floor as both cousin and brother had abandoned their supper in efforts to protect themselves. Meanwhile Lizzy was doing a kind of monologue to the pair and to herself at the same time. The speech that followed went to the rhythm of the smacks she dealt out. 'If-I've-told-you-once-I've told you-bastards-a-thousand-times-I-don't-want-any-arguing-at-dinner.' Her temper had snapped and the reaction was to attack.

'It wiz hur Mammy, she's a weirdo,' Sammy shouted from somewhere beneath my mother's body.

'Shut-the fuck-up-while-am-hitting-yae, ya fucking pest of hell!' Lizzy responded, as she continued to smack Sammy. Sandra it seemed knew to keep quiet and take the beating. She knew it would be over quicker if she curled up in a ball and stayed quiet.

I don't recall exactly how many times scenes like this happened in our house when I was growing up, but I know it was a lot. I know that, as a child, I felt the emotional impact of this scene and others like it so deeply that as I retell it I can feel the whole thing again. Every last sensation of the harshness and reality of the moment becomes clear in my mind and fills me. I feel like I am transported back to that precise time and place.

When Lizzy eventually let them both go, she hurried off to the kitchen to get a cloth and dustpan to clean the mess. She was talking loudly, largely to herself again. While she was out of the room, Sandra sort of straightened herself up. Her face was red and her hair looked a mess, but then she turned to Sammy and just burst into hysterical laughter. She couldn't stop and she had a really loud laugh which was highly infectious. She dropped to the floor on her knees and tears were soon running down her face. She was laughing so heartily that her shoulders were shaking and at times it seemed like she had stopped breathing before she would let out another loud burst of laughter. She looked at me and I remember laughing with her though I have no idea why, perhaps it was a release of tension? But I was also terrified that if Lizzy came back in and saw us it might set her off again. But Sandra just kept laughing and laughing and she got worse when Sammy, who didn't get the joke, shouted at her, 'You are a fucking nutcase, ah hate you!' Then he stormed out of the room leaving Sandra and me rolling about the floor in convulsions. It turned out that my mother had mistaken Sandra's laughter for crying and was busy telling my sisters in the other room, that's what would happen to anyone who upset her and they should take heed of her warning.

Of course I can see now that there was a funny side to all of this. As I describe the scene it sounds like *Punch and Judy* or an old slapstick comedy, but, as I say, at the time I was tense with fear. I spent most of my childhood like this, praying the rows would stop or worrying that they would kick off again. I would shrink deep inside myself, and try to zone out, to be anywhere else.

***

There were many fights in our family, but no matter how much they fought internally, they always regrouped when anyone else threatened the family. Even Sammy and Sandra would put their differences aside. Lizzy, of course, was particularly fierce.

The first family fight I was involved in happened when I was only a babe in arms. As my eldest brother Tommy related it, a neighbour from the street we lived in at the time, a big-built woman, was standing outside our flats shouting up at our window one morning. 'Mrs Smith, Mrs Smith, come doon here right noo, ah want tae talk tae you.' Tommy had heard this bawling and realized that it was the mother of a boy he had gotten friendly with. He says he felt his stomach turn because he had been up to no good. My mother was standing on the second landing holding me in her arms while talking to Mrs MacKay, who lived downstairs from us, and wasn't really aware that she was being called out to by this woman: 'Your thieving bastard of a boy has stolen frae ma son. If you don't come doon and bring that fucking thief wae yea am coming up tae drag yae oot, dae yae hear me?' Fighting talk indeed.

My brother knew that there would be trouble the minute my mother got wind of what was happening, so he thought it was best to get in first.

'Ma, there's a wumin oot there shouting that ah've bin steelin. Honest Ma, it wizny me, a swear.' He says that Lizzy stopped her conversation with Mrs MacKay, and was about to speak to him when the noise from outside came bursting into the entrance of our flats.

'Right where is that wee fucking thief, hand him awer tae me.' Then she came charging up the stairs, face bursting bright red with anger. 'Ur you eez ma, by any chance, hiding away in the fucking close scared tae come oot and face me then?' What came next happened fast and without fuss, according to my brother.

'Get yourself tae fuck,' Lizzy responded, then apparently did a half turn with her body and sent out a short jab which caught the woman square on the jaw. The punch put the big woman onto her backside in the corner of the lower landing. Apparently all this happened while Lizzy held me tight with her left arm and still managed to keep her cigarette between her teeth as she spoke. 'My son's no fucking thief, now get tae fuck away from ma hoos unless yae really want me tae put this waen doon and have a real fight.'

Another time, when I was about five years old, I'd been playing football in the garden and had hung my denim jacket up on the neighbour's fence. When the ball was kicked into his garden – yet again – this neighbour showed his irritation by throwing my jacket on the ground, telling me never to kick balls into his garden again. Suddenly, my mother raced out of our back door and instantly felled this man, who was twice her size, with one hefty punch. As he landed on his back with his legs waving in the air, my mother stood over him and ordered him to pick up my jacket which he did ever so meekly. There was never any answering back where my mother was concerned. She was only about 5' 3", but she fought like a man with her fists.

The first battle I was actually involved in took place sometime in 1967. I remember this because I was wearing a school tie, so I must have started at Balornock Primary School. The fight was against another family in our street, the Urquharts.

My sister Betty tells me that it was a Friday evening. She remembers getting ready to go out that night. Betty was a blonde with big blue eyes. She would have been around seventeen. She sang in pubs or clubs at this time and she sometimes entered singing competitions. She took quite some time to sort out her outfit, hairdo and make-up to look the best she could on stage. Remember it was the 1960s and eyelashes alone would have taken at least an hour to fix.

I was playing with a football again, this time in our front garden with my friend Ian Harvey. Nothing seemed to be out of the ordinary. The Harveys lived next door to us at the time and both his mother and my mother were talking while sweeping the path. Suddenly, an older girl call Anna Barr came screaming towards our path.

'Mrs Smith, Mrs Smith, hurry up! Two boys are fighting with Sammy yae better help him they're bigger boyz, it's the Urquharts.'

My cousin Sandra, who was standing at the opened front door smoking a cigarette, heard this too and called to my sister.

'Betty, move, some bastard's hitting oor Sammy, it's they fucking Urquharts.' Then she flicked her cigarette and shot up the path after Lizzy who had already taken off, brush in hand ready to do battle. I was drawn into this, running behind them. Then my brother Jonny came out of nowhere and overtook me heading to the end of the street to where the Urquhart family lived.

A small crowd had gathered on the path to watch Sammy fighting with the two Urquhart brothers. Sammy was only about nine at the time. The Urquhart brothers would have been in their twenties, home from work. Strange to think but people did things like this then. They gathered around a fight and watched like spectators, sometimes even calling out encouragement and such. Anyhoo, if memory serves it didn't look like my older brother was getting beat up at all. If anything he seemed to be holding his own, but two against one was never fair and by the time I got there all of the Urquhart family were now out of their front door and there were as many of them as there were of us, if not more.

Lizzy and Sandra headed straight for the Urquharts' house

and Sandra grabbed hold of the mother, wrestling the woman to the ground and calling out, 'Lizzy do yae want a punch at her?' Lizzy meanwhile ran into the kitchen, grabbed a frying pan and hit one of the sons in the face with it, while addressing the mother, 'Look at the state of this fuckin' frying pan you dirty, filthy whore!'

Then out of nowhere I got grabbed by the tie and spun round by the youngest Urquhart, Cathy, who was just a year older than me. So my first fight was to be with a girl. She was now choking me and ripping my hair out at the same time. As I remember it, it was Betty who saved me. She came running into the fight fully dressed in nightclub get-up, lacquered hairdo and in full make-up – only to have a bucket full of filthy water thrown over her by another Urquhart, drenching her from head to foot and causing her to scream out in a loud shrill tone. The whole episode was brought to a sudden close when the police arrived. Everyone was pulled apart and the two warring families were separated. No one was badly injured, just a couple of bruises here and there and some hair was left standing up, particularly mine, I recall. I also remember that my tie was somewhat tighter, but all-in-all it was sorted because no one wanted to grass up anyone to the police . . . Both mothers were given a caution and a severe reprimand by a police sergeant who obviously knew that there were far too many people to fit into his small van. The real loss was Betty's hairdo and make-up. Opportunity wasn't going to be knocking for her that night.

Again, we all laugh when we think back to these times because of how ridiculous it must have looked, but we lived in a place and a time when differences were sorted out like this.

My poor dad often never knew the half of what went on

while he was at work. By the time he came home at night everything had settled down. Mother would tell us all not to tell him, that we should give him some peace and quiet to eat his supper. Did he think we were all little angels? I'm sure not. But where my mother was very volatile, dad was much more thoughtful. My mother was a fierce, protective force, but my dad was grounded, strong and courageous so you couldn't help but feel safe when he was around you. You were also more respectful. When he came in we all shut up. It was dad who would make us learn our homework and check it before we went to bed. He taught us all how to tie our ties for school and how tell the time and all the things a good dad does. He told us stories about his time in the Navy and all the places he had seen, filling our imaginations with exotic images which made for good dreams and contented sleeps. Yes, our dad was a good man.

Sometimes he would sit me on his knee and sing little Scottish ditties. I remember the smell of Brylcreem and of work – overalls and the smell of oil. Even though I was put to bed earliest he always gave me a bit of his time before I went to sleep. I also have good memories of my dad taking me and my two older brothers Jonny and Sammy out for day trips to the coast in Ayrshire and on boat trips down the River Clyde in the summertime or on bank holidays. He loved to make his children happy and till the day he died, all the children in our family adored him. I'm sure he wasn't a saint – in fact I know he wasn't – but he had some good values that he tried to pass on.

Unlike my mother, my father always tried to find diplomatic solutions. For instance, if Sammy was in a fight, my dad would take him to the parents of the other boy and they would talk about what happened and try to sort things out. If there was still a matter unsettled he would ask the boys if they wanted to settle it in a fair fist fight in front of both sets of parents. This normally dissuaded the boys as neither wanted to lose in front of their parents.

Another thing that comes to mind when I look back at my early childhood was how clean and well decorated our home was. My father was a great builder and decorator, a jack of all trades and master of many. He had modernized our house in Mansel Street and neighbours would love to come in and look at how he had lowered our ceiling and installed spotlights and built a fireplace which also had fancy inset lighting. Both my parents were proud when it came to their home and they could get visibly puffed up when people complimented them on it.

In my mother's eyes to have a good clean home was everything and she spent much of her time everyday cleaning it and I do mean cleaning it. I'm sure there were hospitals that weren't as hygienic as 97 Mansel Street. I believe this was because she came from such a poor background with little or nothing in her life by way of material things. If you are extremely poor, cleanliness is one of the only advantages you can have over other poor families. My mother would spend hours scrubbing the front doorstep. It seemed she was forever battling to push back a tide of filth that sloshed in through the front door, particularly when it was raining. In the great industrial city of Glasgow even the rain seemed black.

2

The Gorbals, Gangs And Guts

Both my parents were born in 1926 in the Gorbals. It was here on the south bank of the river Clyde that successive waves of immigrants, Irish, Jews and later Indians stepped off the boats and settled, looking for work in the factories and dockyards. My mother, Elizabeth Davis was born in Crown Street on 4 August and about fifty yards away in Ballater just twenty-two days later, Samuel Turtin Smith was born. My mother once said of my father, 'That wee bastard has been following me since just after I was born, I don't think I'll ever fuckin' get rid of him.' Well not for a very long time, Lizzy.

Although they began their life in such close proximity, their worlds couldn't have been further apart. My father was brought up in a Protestant family. Samuel and Joanne, my grandparents both died before I was born. They shared a two-bedroom flat with their eight children, dad being the seventh and second youngest. His parents had good standards of living compared to many other families in the area at the time. It might seem deprived, all those people in one house, but their situation was much better than that of most families in the Gorbals in the twenties and thirties.

On the rare occasions he chose to open up about his child-hood, my father spoke warmly of his parents. His mother had died when he was quite young, but his memories of her were of a good-natured, wholesome woman who liked to tell her children about her family's connections to the Highlands of Scotland. I can still remember the affectionate tone of my father's voice when he spoke about his mother. After her death in the early 1930s my grandfather remarried a woman named Kate, who if I recall properly was referred to as Auld Kate.

My dad really loved his father and looked up to him because he believed in hard work and good family values. Auld Sammy wanted all his children to learn and study as much as they could, considering how little good education was on offer in the poverty-stricken Gorbals at that time. Back then schooling was really just the basic three Rs (Reading, Writing and Arithmetic), but that was a good foundation which my grandad added to by encouraging all his children to read out loud after dinner. He made sure that his children passed their exams and qualifications at school, which was a kind of honour then. This experience of being taught by his father meant that my dad felt the need to inspire his own family in much the same way when it came to learning.

Men of my dad's generation worked twelve hour shifts of truly hard physical work, six days a week. Added to that was the time it took them to cycle or even walk to work and back each day. Yet my dad still found time to enjoy sitting with his children, going over all their lessons. I honestly never remember my father saying he was tired or exhausted. I believe he would have liked to have been more present in family life. He loved children and was happy to help or play with us, but his first priority was to make sure he worked hard enough to provide for us. So, although he wasn't always physically there, the effect of his presence in our lives was a major influence.

In the Gorbals, many people had never learned to read or write and would never have known tenderness or love, let alone a good regular square meal or hot bath. But dad's family were good, decent folk, people who made the most of their lot and all did reasonably well in life.

My mother, well, she had a very different start. According to the stories she shared with us, most of her memories as a child were of hardship. There was no great stability in her early life. Her family never stayed in one home for very long before being moved on somewhere else. There were some highs that she talked about as she got a little older, but more lows and a life that ran very differently from ours.

Mum's family were Irish Catholics. Her parents were Bernhard Davis and Sarah Riley. Lizzy was the second eldest child and one of five. She had an older brother called Barney, one younger sister Sadie and two younger brothers John and Michael.

My grandparents on my mother's side of the family were tempestuous, and their marriage broke up after my grandfather spent some time in prison for something we were never told about. If the stories about my grandfather's young life are to be believed, he appears to have been a bit of a hard man, a streetfighter who fought for money and who was involved in robberies and safe blowing. Bernhard was a very tall, good-looking, well-built guy, something of a dandy in his beautiful Crombie coats and silk cravats, who caught the eye of many of the wrong type of women in the Gorbals.

Lizzy said Bernhard came from surprisingly good people who lived in one of the better parts of Glasgow. She remembered several occasions when members of his family had come round to try to help with money and gifts when Bernhard was in prison. My grandfather sounds like a black sheep who turned his back on the stability of a very decent upper-working-class family in exchange for a wild life with my granny.

Sarah Riley, my grandmother, came from Irish Travellers, I believe, and though several members of my family have tried to trace her roots, it's almost as if she had never existed in this world.

The only time I ever witnessed my mother cry was when she told us stories of her mother slogging her guts out for a couple of shillings just so they could have coal for the fire and food for a few days. It broke my heart to hear that.

Sarah Riley was a small, good-natured, fine-looking woman who wore her mousy brown hair very short for those times. Her main features were her striking high cheekbones and big, almond-shaped, dark brown eyes. She was charismatic and had the Irish gift of blarney. She was also as hard as nails. Some stories talk of her knocking men out by head-butting them and once she ran into the middle of the Orange Parade as it passed through the Gorbals and tore the earrings out of a Protestant woman's ears. Then she fought with Orangemen leading the walk until she was arrested by the police.

My vague recollection of older relations coming to our home when I was young was that they always seemed to light up when they talked about Sarah. I can always remember thinking I would have loved to have met her. (I did in a way but that's another story which I will tell later.) She was clearly adored by all of her children and whenever my mother got together with her sister and brothers or with her cousins, the conversation often turned to Sarah and how hard she worked to provide for her young family. There was always an array of emotions, happy, sad and a little bit of real magic too.

She made money to provide for her kids by cleaning people's houses from early in the morning till late at night. Lizzy said she would scavenge things on rubbish tips, clean them up and walk the streets selling them from a bag made out of a blanket slung over her shoulder and tied together with a bit of old rope or take them to the old flea market in Glasgow (the Brigget) which was where many of the Irish traders and hawkers bought and sold to make a living.

Mum also said that her mother worked all through the night sometimes and would boil-wash clothes and bedding. Then she would press everything to perfection with an old solid iron which had to be heated on the open coal fire; in this way, she made everything she was selling look like new. It might seem like nothing nowadays, but then neighbours praised her for how spotless and meticulous her wares were and how clean she kept her home and family. Back then to be complimented on such things in the Gorbals was a high honour indeed. I can still hear my mother say, 'My mother's white-wash wiz the talk of the street, sometimes people said it wiz that white it was blue. Yea don't huv tae huv money to be clean.' Lizzy drummed that into us. We all heard her say many times that her mother's little humble flat was immaculate and how fresh it smelled. In fact it wasn't a flat as such, just a room with a kitchen sink (known as a kitchen flat) which housed all six of them, but as mother always proudly boasted, 'There wiz nothing worth stealing in it, but it wiz the cleanest fuckin' hoose in the Gorbals.'

In those days the Gorbals was one of the most overcrowded places in Britain. The overcrowding was so extreme in this small area that there were three times more people sharing a room in Gorbals homes than anywhere else in the city of Glasgow. All this deprivation and yet people still made their lives worse by cultivating religious bigotry.

Protestants and Catholics pursued great rivalries throughout the city of Glasgow, but it was in the Gorbals where most of the street battles were fought. Gangs would attack using weapons like hammers, hatchets and open razors. This was a weapon that became synonymous with the Gorbals gangs and thugs of the day. Much was made of it at the time in books like *No Mean City* and *The Gorbals Story*. The hatred between Protestants and Catholics was also fuelled in the terraces of the football stadiums of Rangers and Celtic. The Gorbals was located in between the two football grounds which meant rival fans naturally collided there. Often this ended with the two sides brawling in the streets on a Saturday night. I remember as a child once sitting on a bus which became surrounded by rival gangs of supporters hacking at each other with steak knives. Sadly, the poorly educated people of the Gorbals at this time genuinely thought that this hatred and ridiculous behaviour had something to do with religion.

I truly wonder with all this around them, how ma and pa actually got together.

My parents met through my dad's sister, Aunt Agnes. At the age of seventeen Aggy, as she was known to us, had a dream of being part of the Moccasin Girls, a dance troupe that played in theatres all around Scotland at that time. Lizzy shared that dream, even though they sat on different sides of the religious fence.

It was both girls' desire to get out of the Gorbals and, of course, dress up in pretty show clothes and be seen by all the young servicemen. There it was, two young girls with the same shared wish to dance on stage began their friendship in the backyards of the dreary, rat-infested, filthy, religiously-bigoted streets of *Les Gorbals*.

My mother was a year younger than Aggy, who had already had dance lessons and boasted that she could kick her own height and do the splits. I can just hear mother's husky voice now sarcastically speaking out of the corner of her mouth, lip curled for full effect, 'I bet she fucking could.' Lizzy loved any reason to take a cheap shot at her best friend. They really *were* friends – that's just a Glaswegian trait, to slag off your best pals. But you wouldn't let anyone else do it and if it wasn't for my mother's friendship with Aunt Aggy, my parents would probably have never met.

At sixteen, my mother was a good-looking young woman with dark, wavy, auburn hair neatly fashioned off her pretty face and strong green eyes. She followed fashion as much as she could afford to. Lizzy always liked nice things. In her teens she helped her mother with cleaning and selling clothes in the Brigget, doing whatever she needed to do to save money to buy whatever latest clothes were available to buy – or even make when she had to. It was 1943 and there wasn't much of anything going around and even less in the kitty to pay for things.

Lizzy Davis loved to go to the cinema with her new friend Aggy Smith and dream of being part of the glamour and glitz of the high-kicking girls who were dazzling them on the big screen. Mum shared her name with one of the biggest Hollywood stars of the day – Bette Davis – who like my mother was born Elizabeth Davis. Over the years, people have suggested that there were other similarities between them . . .

I can still remember how my mother's eyes would come

to life and how she'd laugh when she told us stories from those days. She described how all the dancers would darken their legs with old, stewed tea and draw lines up the back of their legs as they couldn't afford stockings. On other occasions they would only have enough hair lacquer to do the front of their hair so they could never turn their backs on the audience when exiting the stage without risk of revealing the flat patch at the back of their heads.

It sounded like there was a great deal of fun being had even in such a depressing time. When reminiscing, Lizzy's mouth would sometimes twist to the side, usually whilst letting out billows of smoke for added effect, and then some catty comment would come out about auntie, 'I mean, she wasn't a bad dancer considering how knock-kneed she was. I was always worried the daft cow would trip herself up.' Or, 'She wasn't bad looking if you were sitting at the back of the theatre.' But mum always said that Aggy gave as good as she got.

I found it hard to imagine my mother on a stage dancing and showing off her legs, which she always said were the best shaped and most admired in the chorus line. The Lizzy I knew was self-conscious about herself and thought women who showed too much skin were sluts and whores. She could also be very funny though. As she did the housework she ran a sort of commentary on goings-on in the street. I can picture her with her cheeks all ruddy from merriment, hands on hips, wagging her head, 'I'm not as crazy as that fucking whore down the street.' And part of it was that she was a great mimic and mime, 'Look at her standing there as if she's shit herself!' she'd say, striking a pose.

It was a lively, funny, lovely young showgirl that my father fell in love with. Lizzy said he used to lurk around the theatres waiting for her to finish so he could ask if he could walk her home and offer to light her cigarettes.

Dad signed up for the Royal Navy in 1944 and Lizzy tried to join the Wrens, but failed the written test. Instead she quickly joined the Auxiliary Territorial Service (ATS) and went on tour as a dancer, sometimes singing in the chorus. My mother had a very strong singing voice – imagine Shirley Bassey mixed with George Melly. Loud and deep. When dad was sent off on his first tour of active duty she and my father kept contact for the next year by letter. When he returned in the spring of 1945 they married. It was on 7 April. I remember my son asking my mother when she was in her eighties, 'Granny, can you remember how my grandad proposed to you?' Lizzy thought for a minute, made a kind of sniffing noise as she looked like she was trying to remember word for word, then said: 'He told me he was going away for another two years and he wanted me to marry him before going back to the war. I just said, "Aye, if yeah want tae." ' It's like a scene from *Gone with the Wind*.

Like most young men during the war, dad wanted to have a sweetheart both to write to and come home to. He said that he just knew that she was the right one for him. He must have liked them feisty. He told me he bought a ring from the pawn shop in Oxford Street in the Gorbals that morning, all they could afford at the time. Then he and my mother and two witnesses went to the registry office in Glasgow to tie the knot. My father says that his biggest fear of that day was not about he and my mother getting married, but more that his father, a devout Protestant and follower of the Orange Order, would have to meet Lizzy's mother, a diehard Catholic who wasn't afraid to show it. I've already mentioned how dear grandmama sometimes behaved towards people connected with the Orange Order, and it would seem that for all my grandpapa was better educated, he used to display paintings of King Billy on his white horse in his window whenever there was a Catholic march in the Gorbals.

In the couple of years since my mother and father had met they hadn't really got to know each other's parents, realizing that the less said about a Catholic and a Protestant going out with one another the better. Back then many such relationships were forbidden. Sometimes when one parent or other found out, there wasn't much you could do other than run away. However, on the day, Sarah and Auld Sammy actually put their differences aside and shared a drink and a few laughs. The marriage seemed to be getting off to a good start, which was just as well because my father only had a couple of days on shore before heading off to sea again, and now word got back to Lizzy that her elder brother had just been arrested.

Her wedding day should have been a very happy day for my mother. It should have been the first day of the rest of her new life and I'm sure that's what she thought as she and my father shared their first night together in the recessed bed in her mother's one-roomed kitchen flat, alongside Sarah and her three youngest children, who were sleeping next to her. I have tried so many times to imagine the dreams and thoughts that my mother, the good-looking young showgirl must have had at that moment.

I wonder if she thought about her career on stage, or of some of the places dad would travel to, places that poor people from the Gorbals could never hope to visit aside from wartime. She probably thought about getting her own home with my dad at the end of the war and starting her own family.

I always hope that the feelings of those dreams were never totally washed away. She was only nineteen and this was her wedding night.

My dad tells what happened next like this.

He says that he was lying next to my mother and, though there were so many people crammed into such a small place, there was an intense stillness, a quiet he says he will never forget. Lizzy's mother, Sarah had a real smoker's cough and at some point it dawned on him that the constant coughing had stopped and he wasn't sure in his semi-sleep state for how long, but in his own words: 'I don't know how I knew, but something was wrong with that woman. My whole body went rigid for a wee minute, then I woke your mother, who was asleep, and told her that I thought there was something wrang wae her ma.'

My mother seemed to know, too, what my father was sensing. They both jumped out of bed and past the curtain that separated them from the rest of the room and moved quickly over to Sarah. It was my dad who tried to rouse her. This woke up the youngsters by her side and my mother took them outside the front door onto the street. John, Sadie and Michael were very young, still half asleep and wondering what was going on, as Lizzy tried to comfort them and tell them things would be ok.

Later Lizzy told me that the sound of my dad's voice saying, 'Sarah, Sarah, come on now, wake up', haunted her for years because she knew in her heart at that moment that her mother wasn't going to wake up. Her mother was usually awake for at least twenty hours of every day cooking, cleaning and washing clothes to sell for pennies in the market. Her mother took all her children wherever she went and never, never let them out of her sight. All Lizzy's instincts told her that her mother was the lightest sleeper and for her not to respond while her kids were being taken away from her was a bad sign. This terrifying thought now filled my mother's mind on her wedding night. It must have felt like every hope and dream she ever dared to have was slipping like water through her open fingers. She had only been a wife for a matter of a few short hours, but on the night of her wedding she became a mother of three.

Sarah had choked to death on her own vomit. She wasn't a heavy drinker, but that evening she had celebrated with her daughter and in-laws and who knows, maybe the poor woman was just so exhausted that the alcohol was enough to knock her out. My parents rarely talked about that night when I was young. I think they had both suffered the sort of shock that penetrates the very soul and it is natural that you try to suppress it. Many years on when I was in my thirties, dad once shared with me that when he had looked at Sarah's face he had known immediately that she was dead. He said that her skin was a green colour and that her throat had swollen to double its normal size.

What fascinated me about our conversation was he said that when he was able to look back at the situation some years later, he remembered that something bizarre like an inner voice had woken him. This was not the kind of thing my father spoke about, voices or visions and such. No, he wasn't that kind of person, but something, or someone without a body woke him to find his mother-in-law of several hours, dead in a bed just a few feet away from where he lay.

Everything changed for the young Lizzy after her mother's

death. My father was only given an extra two days compassionate leave from the Navy in order to attend the funeral; then he had to go back to sea. This left my mother with the burden of bringing up her younger brothers and sister, all still of school age and grieving the loss of their mother who had been the centre of their entire universe. How did she cope with this and her own grief for the loss of her mother and, in a sense, her marriage too? She told my sister many years later that she was never certain if my father would come back to her after the war. She always believed that if he survived, he wouldn't want to take on the responsibility of her younger siblings. She obviously didn't know my father back then.

I have long believed that this is when my mother became angry, truly angry in a way that is deep-seated and cold. This kind of anger is very different from rage which is hot and burns out. A real cold aggression can sit in the depth of the soul for years. My mother used to say that she hated God: 'God, that bastard don't talk tae me aboot any fucking God. I curse that bastard and hope his heaven turn to hell when ees no looking.' She wasn't kidding about this and as for things like Protestant versus Catholic, it didn't matter now. She would never enter a church of any type again. She must have hated life and didn't dare to dream of happiness any more.

She once told me that it was unlucky to wish for nice things because if you do, she said, bad things will happen. How sad is that?

After her mother's death Lizzy became tough and hardened. I suppose she had to. She was a nineteen-year-old woman living in a room with three children aged twelve, ten and eight. Her husband was at sea, her older brother was now in prison and her father had abandoned them years before. With no one to pray to she would have to become a realist and believe in her own abilities to succeed, no matter what life threw at her.

Some people become broken-spirited and crumble when they face tragedy. Others, like my mother seem to become charged and stand waiting defiantly for the next bout of hard times to come and try to see them off. I've heard it said that the golden eagle will not shy away from a storm but instead fly headlong into it. My mother was a bit like that.

There was a story she used to tell from the time when the family was still living in Portugal Street, the same small flat where her mother had died. Lizzy was on her hands and knees cleaning the wax cloth flooring with an old fashioned scrubbing brush when she heard screams and shouts from the street. This in itself wasn't that strange, but what happened next was. Suddenly, she heard a loud noise and looked up. She didn't know what was happening but out of nowhere a gigantic object darkened her front window momentarily and then CRASH . . . A horse's head was suspended above her, blood spewing out everywhere. She screamed at the top of her lungs not knowing what to expect next. Then the animal bled to death in front of her very eyes.

It seems that the horse had been pulling a rag-and-bone man's cart and escaped its stays, panicked and ended up crashing through her front window.

Seconds later there were crowds of people in the small room all trying to help release the beast from the shards of broken glass that impaled it.

The flat had once been a shop and the window had a huge single pane, so imagine how much that would have cost to repair even in those days. People didn't have home insurance back then – certainly not in the Gorbals. But some of the locals came to her rescue and replaced the glass with wood at least to keep out the cold.

When my father heard of this he sent back the wages he had saved so that Lizzy could have the glass replaced which she did, but not until the following year. She chose to spend the money on food and clothes. I remember her saying, 'We needed provisions more than a view of that fucking dump.' Ever the pragmatist my mother.

During the time my father was off in the Navy my mother must have got into countless fights with women and men in the Gorbals trying to protect her brothers and sisters from some of the characters that hung around. She told us that her brother John, who was just twelve, but looked mature for his age was running a card school with some guys in their late teens. She found out about it at the last minute. This card game attracted many undesirables, but one young man who would have been my mother's age, caught John cheating and lunged at him, grabbing at his shoulders. Then he pushed John against the wall of the tenement close beside my mother's flat. Lizzy heard the loud shouts and shot out towards the sound of the commotion. Before she knew it she'd thrown a punch at the older guy knocking him backwards and then rather than wait for him to get his balance, she fired a second and third until he was on the ground. John protested his innocence to Lizzy as the guy called him a cheat from his position on the ground, but my mother didn't care who was right or wrong. Her heart was pumping and she knew she couldn't let anyone hurt her younger brother. As she stood rigid, looking around the close area at the other young men, keeping her fists clenched, she was still fired-up and ready for anyone else who wanted to have a go at her or her brother.

There was no comeback and she ordered the young men out of her street before turning to talk to her brother.

'Were you fucking cheating thoose guys John?' she demanded.

'Aye a did cheat Lizzy. I'm sorry, but look a wun loads a money for yae.' My mother said she couldn't be angry at him. She loved her brother and would literally have died for him. The boys he was cheating were probably doing the same thing, only he was better at it. She scraped some of the coins from his hand, allowing him to keep the rest, and playfully smacked the back of his head. Uncle John told me not long before he died that this account my mother told me was true, except that the real money he'd won was in his sock and Lizzy never ever found out about it – and word of fights travelled fast.

Some neighbours felt sorry for her, and even though they were all poor, many offered whatever little help they could. Lizzy was always grateful for that and never forgot those who had extended the hand of friendship to her and her family. It was this kind of street support that I also loved in my parents. Both were quick to help in whatever way they could when someone in our street was in trouble. I believe that most people who lived during the wars have inherited this sense of community, of being in it together.

***

The war was over but it was still a dire time. Our father was not one of the ones who returned early, but many men who did come back to the Gorbals must have felt they had just left one war zone only to return to another. The crime rate had escalated. People were stealing what they could out of pure desperation. Luckily my mother knew some right thugs in the 1940s. For many families the only way they would get decent food was to obtain it from the local gangs who ran the underworld. This must have been reflected throughout the country at this time, I imagine.

One day my mother marched into the house of the woman her father was living with at the time. Lizzy went round to have it out with her father face to face. She wanted to know if he was willing to help her out with cash for his children. People in the streets had been talking, saying that he was earning money on the side and that it was terrible his daughter had to provide for her brothers and sister on her own. The family living at this house was called Lyons, a big, hard family with many connections, if you know what I mean. Never one to be put off by numbers, Lizzy fronted up to the woman in charge of the house. Kate Lyons was also a very formidable woman by all accounts. Reportedly she said to my mother, 'Either you are stupid and you don't know who I am Lizzy Davis, or yur pretty brave, hen.' Lizzy lifted her fist to punch her but the men in the living room intervened and pulled her away.

My mum says that she remembered being really frightened because the people in this house were all notorious gang members, crooks and hard-cases. She described them as 'the lowest of the fucking low'. To my mother's great relief, Grandad Bernhard came out from a room in the back of the small house. Kate Lyons gave him money for my mother and her family and she told Bernhard that his daughter was tough and big-hearted and that she should be respected.

From then he started to visit from time to time. He would bring things for the family which made it easier on Lizzy who, like her own mother before her, was cleaning houses and taking in washing. The little flat in Portugal Street was spotless, just as Sarah had kept it, and Lizzy was managing to feed and clothe her brothers and sister – but of course she longed for the day my dad would come back. And though he wrote about coming back to her, she could never be sure. My sister Betty told me that Lizzy shared with her that her marriage had never been consummated before he left and she was willing to offer my dad an annulment if he wanted it. I'm sure she hoped that her worst fears wouldn't happen, but like she said herself, wishing for good things only brought bad luck.

On the morning when my dad got back to the Clyde Grandfather Bernhard was standing at the Gorbals Cross, at the junction of Gorbals Street and Ballater Street, two minutes from my mother's flat. He saw sailors walking over the bridge from Clyde Street to the Gorbals and recognized my dad. He ran round to warn his daughter. 'Lizzy, Sammy Smith's coming over the bridge, quick come and meet him!' But she didn't. Instead, she stood at the end of her street waiting to see if he would turn right and come to her or turn left towards his father's house in Ballater Street. He stopped at the Cross. Children were asking what he had in his kit bag. 'Mr, Mr, huv yae goat any chocolate? Mr did yae bring back fags or things fae abroad?' My dad turned right into Norfolk Street. When Lizzy saw this she went back to the flat, straightened herself up to her full 5' 3", lit a cigarette and took up full pose in the doorway. 'Sammy, before you say anything else I want tae tell you that I'm bringing up my brothers and sister and if you don't want tae be a part oh that, then don't put a foot over this doorstep. My life is very different fae wit it wiz when you went away, but if yae still want me then they come with me, so it's up tae you if yae walk oor this doorstep.' Then she hung her head and looked down at the spotless clean grey sandstone step between them.

3

The Secrets Of 1969

It was the late sixties and every room in our apartment in Mansel Street in north Glasgow, had carpets which my mother loved to clean with her latest device. The carpet sweeper made a type of loud snoring sound as it was pushed and pulled all over our flat every morning and night or when anyone dropped crumbs on the mock Axminster. In the far left corner of our living room sat a big black and white TV, which was set in a walnut-effect cabinet with one of those aerials sitting on top that is a half-sphere of hard plastic with two thin metal antennas sticking out like a V. But the one thing that we kids loved most in our highly colourful living room was the cream leatherette, stud-fronted cocktail bar.

Browns, yellows and oranges, stripes, spots and swirls were in when it came to décor. All of those groovy colours and patterns oozed over the floor, walls and furniture. Then, of course, there was dad's hand-constructed stone fireplace with red inset lights to set it off. In 1969 the world was, of course, a wee bit psychedelic. People who wanted to get high, should have just looked at the patterns and colours on the walls and floors of people's front rooms.

I remember lots more about my life from this time on. I reckon that most children are not fully connected to their conscious minds for several years, that our consciousness, like any part of our being, has to adapt to this physical world and grow and get stronger before it becomes fully formed. That is perhaps why, when we are very young, memories are hard to pinpoint. Perhaps it was for these sorts of reasons that in this year, at the age of seven, I began to feel much more present in my body and in the world. My memory of events in my life and of those around me is, from that point on, much stronger and easier to recall.

I distinctly remember the end of 1968 and the beginning of 1969 because my eldest brother Tommy came back to live with us again. His arrival between Christmas and New Year was most welcomed by the whole family. Tommy had always been fun, very high-spirited and a true Glasgow character. Tommy being home for Christmas was as good as having a visit from Santa Claus. He's the type of person who it's easy to make laugh and he's just as capable of making others laugh too.

His absence had been a mystery to me. Whenever I asked about him – 'Mammy, when's Tommy coming hame, heez been away fur ages?' – my mother would usually answer, 'Shushed noo, and don't ask me aboot Tommy again, and never ask aboot yer brother if people are in this hoos. Noo, get oot an play wae yur brothers and shut up asking aboot things wee boyz shoodny be asking aboot.' One of those family secrets I would get used to . . .

Tommy always had fascinating things to talk about, places he'd been, people he'd met, his interests; he'd always enthused about life. My brother was now twenty-one and, as I learned many years later, the reason he'd been away was because he'd been sent to borstal, which kind of changed him. There was one time he was supposed to watch me for the day and instead of staying at home with me, he took me into town. I can still remember really clearly everything about that trip.

It began when we went on the number four bus which came through Mansel Street. We sat upstairs and Tommy was smoking. I remember this because I kept watching how he smoked. It was different from how my mother smoked. Tommy held his cigarette with his index finger wrapped round the tip, whereas Lizzy held hers at the very tips of her index and middle finger in a very tense manner, which made it look like it could fall at any second. Strange, the things children notice.

The bus drew up outside a huge grey building in town at the top of Cathedral Street. Tommy told me that Betty and Sandra worked in that building. It was called Collins, a publishers and both my sister and cousin were bookbinders. Our bus trip moved on to Bath Street at the top of town where it eventually stopped. Tommy then took me into a record shop. I will never forget how he sat me in a kind of big glass box, a sound booth. He then handed me a small bottle of pop which he took from his pocket. It felt like I was getting a reward. Then the expression on his face changed to a very stern look before he dished out the following instructions: 'Noo listen Gordon, I've goat tae go oot fur a wee while. Ah wont be long so jeest you sit here and don't move awright. The man ower there will keep eez eye on yae, remember, I'll only be a few minutes.' I got the message; he was just about to abandon me in town while he went and attended to some business or other. Something a seven-year-old shouldn't know about. The good thing was he'd given me a lemonade and put big soft padded head-phones over my ears which he adjusted to fit me before he went running off.

What a strange moment for me. I had no idea where I was, just sitting in a glass room with my ears covered. My mother would have killed him if she knew what he'd done – or if I'd told her – hence the lemonade and oversized cans over my small head I suppose, but then something happened that I had never experienced before. A sound filled my entire body with a beat and rhythm that blended with my soul and caused my pulse to accelerate off the scale. It was an extraordinary sensation, the memory of which has stayed with me to this day. It was the intro to Marvin Gaye's hit record of the time, 'Heard it through the Grapevine' and it was playing into my ears louder than I had ever heard music before. I really, really liked what this felt like. Talk about having your mind blown, wow! Even now, hearing the first few bars of that intro on the radio or TV gives me goose bumps. I can feel myself drift back in time to that music shop in Glasgow and the old sound booths. This is something I will always thank Tommy for, because this wonderful, early experience grew through my life into a great love of soul music and it began right at that moment.

I know Tommy was my brother but even so, I think he was kind of cool back then. I'm sure lots of people thought the same. He always had lots of friends and good-looking girls around him. He seemed to attract joy and sometimes mischief, I suppose. It didn't matter to me because I always loved to be around Tommy. He was and still is, full of life. The only thing that changes about him is his age.

The dynamic in our house was just about to change, though. People were always coming and going back then and the sleeping arrangements in our home were like a game of musical chairs. It would all depend on who came home, or if any other waif or stray moved in for a night. If Tommy was in, for example, he would be in Jonny's bed, Jonny would share with Sammy and I would be at the bottom of Joan's bed. I think you get the picture, but a couple of things happened in quick succession around early 1969 and as a result I ended up having the couch in our living room to myself for a while, luxury indeed.

Betty had got married the year before in 1968 and had moved in with her husband, Joe. By the time the bells rang in the New Year she was ready to drop at any moment and in fact she delivered a baby boy in the wee small hours on 3 January. Again, this was a time when I wasn't supposed to ask questions, certainly not when they might be about babies and how my sister had got pregnant. Such questions would have gone beyond a telling-off from mother, could even result in a smack and being put to bed for the night, well until someone needed it, then I would be lifted onto the couch.

I don't remember much about my sister's wedding, but I do remember a party in the flat above ours. Joe Flood, Betty's husband lived above us. A small get-together in the Flood's house was all the two families could have afforded, I suppose. I remember being in our home with my brothers, Sammy and Jonny. My Uncle John's children were there too. They were the same ages as Sammy and Jonny, and I recall that we were all having tremendous fun playing with the coats that people had been left piled on our couch. Five kids can have a lot of fun with a big pile of coats, dressing up and hiding under them, or putting cigarette butts and sugar in the pockets for a laugh. Our Sammy even made a few bob as well as some good finds to sell-on after robbing them of any loose change or other bounty left in pockets.

We were having so much fun that we weren't missing our parents or families at all. Lizzy made sure someone came down every five minutes to check on us. All was well when there was a knock at the door and Sammy opened it to find there was a couple wanting to know where the party was. Sammy thought at first they had come to the wrong door, but it turned out my cousin Mick, who was just coming down the stairs, knew the couple. Their names were Margaret and Alec Marshall and it turned out they were friends of my Uncle John. Mick told them to go to the flat above and that seemed to be that. Only it wasn't.

The Marshalls were a bit of a joke in the neighbourhood. Alec was a small, rather weedy, wheedling man who never had a job but ran errands for my Uncle John. We used to say he was like a wart on Uncle John's arse. His wife Margaret was much bigger than him and used to boss him around and complain about him. The Marshalls had not been invited to the party. Mrs Flood, Joe's mother didn't know who they were. She met them at the top of the stairs and wouldn't let them in. She thought that they were a couple of gatecrashers and sent them packing; in Glasgow then people often just blagged their way into parties to get a free drink.

Back at our place downstairs we were all having a whale of a time when the front door, which wasn't locked, burst open and Alec came running in calling out in a very high-pitched, almost hysterical tone over his shoulder in the direction of his wife who entered our house behind him roaring.

'Margaret, darlin' I love you, please don't hit me darlin' I love you sweetheart, baby please, no, wait.' This noise just froze all of us from our games as we stopped to watch the shenanigans. Alec, as I mentioned, a small and slenderly built man, was now running around our couch, which was still covered by the mountain of coats, and sounding very out of breath. Margaret, large though she was, was in swift pursuit of him and for a big woman she couldn't half shift.

'Ya skinny wee lying, snake-like bastard, when I get you I'll throttle yae, stop and take it like a man ya fucking eel.' This was gripping, enthralling stuff.

'Darling, honey, baby, please.' His words could have come straight out of a James Brown song, but big Hurricane Margaret was having none of the honey-talk.

'Don't you honey baby me ya wee fucking rat, I'll . . .' and with that she caught him. She caught him right in front of the couch. She swung her big arm at him and hit him with a right upper cut which sent him flying onto the coats. His body tucked under itself and he did a kind of backward roll and landed upside down behind the sofa.

It didn't end there because Margaret hurled her huge frame over the coats moving the couch with her immense power and causing it to fall backwards almost crushing Alec in the process. Margaret was now rolling onto her back as Alec tried to make his escape through our open front window. But Margaret was onto him in an instant and again showed great dexterity as her big chubby hand snapped hold of his skinny ankle. It looked like a bear grabbing a slippery salmon in its big paw. 'Ahhhhhh . . .' Alec screamed and made a noise like a girl as his wife pulled at him. His groin area was now trapped halfway out the window. He had been moving forward only to crash back down on the hard, wooden cill. 'Ahhhhhhhhh . . .' More high pitched screams from Alec – and much laughter from all of the children, who were standing around enjoying the spectacle.

My parents and my Uncle John then appeared in the living room to witness this scene with looks of bewilderment on their faces. Then other people began pouring out of the party to see what was happening. Big Margaret was now pulling herself onto her husband's slight frame which was wriggling beneath her enveloping mass. The presence of the other people in the room must have made Mrs Marshall look back and Alec slid from her grasp. He ended up under our window in the front garden on the nettles. 'What the fuck's going on in here?' Lizzy cried out. But Margaret ignored her and forced herself forward after her husband through the window which opened to its fullest as her upper body went out, her legs flew up in the air, knickers now revealed for all to see. She had obviously decided he needed more of a lesson and she had gone well past the point of shame.

Alec rolled onto his back in the middle of our front lawn and Big Maggs stood over him like a gladiator awaiting the thumbs up or down. We didn't have pay-to-view boxing matches back then, but we honestly didn't need it, did we? Margaret began pummelling him with her big, meaty fore-arms, bingo wings flying until my father arrived behind Margaret and put his arm around her and with a kind of gentle force, escorted her back into the house – through a door this time. 'Sammy, I'm so sorry, but I'm fucking morti-fied, that wee weasle lied tae me; wit a fucking showing-up in front ay awe these people.' Poor Margaret was exhausted by now and needed a drink.

The show was over and so it seemed was the party at the Flood's house. Typical dad, he fixed things and brought everyone back to our house to carry on the party. Even the Marshalls got into the swing of it. All in all, the night was enjoyed by all. It was normal at Glasgow parties in those days to have fights, and if the brawl happened early on then everyone was free to get on with the singing, and that's what happened at this one. Alec sang a song called 'Too Many Chiefs . . . Not

Enough Indians' all the while glaring at his wife with a twisted look of protest on his thin, drawn face. I think Big Margaret retorted by singing 'Who's Sorry Now'.

***

I was to see another example of the way my parents took care of things in the neighbourhood after a family moved in a couple of doors down. I used to play in the street with one of the boys, who was my age. One sunny evening some of us were gathered in the kitchen. Suddenly we heard loud screams coming from outside. It was a woman's voice and she sounded distraught. My father led the way outside and started shouting at two men who had a hold of our neighbour, and were trying to pull her out of her front door. 'Hoy there let her go!' The men were dressed in suits and that should have told us something. Lizzy shot past my father as did my brother Tommy, and between them they smacked both the well-dressed gentlemen. 'Hit a poor defenceless fucking wumin wull yae, ya fucking coward.' Lizzy was shouting at her man as she wrestled him to the ground.

It turned out that our neighbour had got behind with her rent and these guys had been sent to remove her from the premises. Once my father had managed to stop the brawl and make sure no charges would be brought against Lizzy or Tommy, he offered to pay the back rent and give our poor neighbour a chance to sort herself out.

Betty leaving our house was another one of the big changes that took place in 1969. My cousin Sandra, who had lived with us for years also left then, but under very different circumstances.

Glasgow gangs would hang around street corners and sometimes arrange to meet and do battle with gangs from other neighbourhoods. In the north of Glasgow one of the most notorious gangs was called the Springburn Peg. Mansel Street, where we lived, was in an area known as Balornock which was really just an extension of Springburn, so many of the gang members lived around us. Sandra had gotten friendly with one of the gang members, a guy called Sammy Divers. But being originally from the Gorbals, Sandra told the Springburn guys that they wouldn't last a minute if they took on people from there. In fact, she loved to belittle these young men and would even challenge some of them to fight with her. She reckoned that even a Gorbals woman could handle a group of men from Springburn in a fist fight. Although we were all very fond of Sandra because she was funny and kind, she was also very territorial and liked to put on a display of aggression.

She was obviously a bit messed up. She had gotten into trouble in the Gorbals after fighting with boys and had been sent to live with us as a result.

It's quite obvious that she was still heading for trouble, but Sandra knew that we would always be there for her if things got out of hand. She also had many friends in the Gorbals whose names and reputations carried some kind of weight and this is really what probably kept the Springburn boys from reacting to her threats. However, things went a bit too far one night when something Sandra did caused an eruption the repercussions of which sent her running back to the Gorbals; not perhaps because she was scared of the gangs of Springburn, so much as what my mother would do to her after her reckless behaviour.

Betty had just come out of hospital with Stephen, who was

only a couple of weeks old at the time. She was in our house late one Saturday night with her husband Joe and the baby, probably showing him off to my Aunt Sadie, my mother's sister. She was visiting us that night with her husband Abby. I knew it was quite late when everything kicked off because my brothers and me were in our beds. I was sharing with Jonny that night, so someone else must have been scheduled to take the couch. All was well and we could hear the adults talking in the living room when there was the most almighty crash I had ever heard in my young life. It was like a bomb had gone off and the sound of breaking glass rang so loud in my ears that it caused my head to freeze for a moment.

I remember jumping out of bed in complete terror, along with my two brothers. As we pulled the bedroom door back we could see that the adults in our family had already shot out the front door which was wide open and as sometimes happened in our family, when the adults ran, so did we.

As strange as it sounds, I don't recall any of us screaming or crying. We were just stunned into complete silence. Betty was the closest to us. She was at the end of our path looking towards the far end of Mansel Street, and when she saw us behind her she turned and motioned the three of us back up the path and into the house. She looked shocked and we realized that every window in our house had been smashed. Even the small square pane in the top part of the front door was gone. There must have been a full gang of boys positioned at every window with a pole or brick ready to smash simultaneously when the word went out.

I remember the feeling of terror escalating once more when I looked at Betty again when we were all back indoors. She was now cradling her baby, lifting him from the big pram he'd been asleep in. She was shaking like the rest of us,

looking around in bewilderment. She gathered Jonny and me
beside her on the couch, which was one of the few places
free of glass, and tried her best to reassure us. 'Right, ah
want yae awe tae sit doon on the couch and don't move till
I say – ok?' None of us spoke, but Sammy went straight to
the bedroom to get dressed. I don't think Betty wanted to
waste her energy arguing with him. Nothing was going to
stop him from going outside to see what had happened. She
looked exhausted and worried as she cradled Stephen in her
arms before laying him back into the big, blue, high pram.
She then bent forward and began to pick up some of the
bigger pieces of glass that were all around the living room.

I'd experienced fear before, but now I felt something more,
a development. It started with an inner sound like an alarm.
I knew it was inside me and that no one else could hear it,
but it frightened me. It grew louder and louder, far too loud
for me to think or entertain any thoughts or feelings other
than fear.

Betty had told us in no uncertain terms that we were not
to move from the couch till she was sure that it was safe and
all the glass in the living room was cleared. At last, there was
the sound of a loud voice filling our hall and it felt much
better somehow than the sound that shattered every bit of
glass around our house moments earlier. There was a familiar
tone to this voice.

'Bastards, dirty fucking bastards, you should have let me
kill him, Sammy.' It was Sadie's voice we could hear first. 'I
hid ees head in ma hawns, so ah did.'

'Everybody calm doon, the police are ootside.' My father's
voice was loud and strained. The living room door opened
and Lizzy came in. She was silent and that wasn't a good

sign. She had a look on her face of pure rage that says she was ready to kill somebody.

'Ur the kids ok Betty? Keep them there till ah start tae clean this fucking mess up.' She was fuming as she worked to clear the mess in double the speed of my sister.

'Wit happened Ma? Who wiz it, dae yae know yet? Did yae catch them?' Betty was anxiously firing questions at my mother. There were moans coming from outside in the hall and then I could hear my father talking quietly to someone. 'You're going nowhere, son, till you tell me who you are and why you and your gang did this, dae yae hear me?' My father had caught one of the gang who had been responsible for smashing our windows. He was holding him around the neck in a kind of half-nelson and the young guy was stuck. It seemed dad had dragged him like this from the far end of the street where he captured the thug. He was lucky it was my father who was restraining him and not Lizzy . . .

The rest of that night became a blur for me and somehow I don't remember even falling asleep, but I do clearly recall the next morning. It looked like all of Mansel Street was outside our house, standing outside there looking at the boards which my father and Joe had put in place over all of our windows, front and back and sides.

'What happened Gordon?' Cathy Urquhart was demanding to know. 'My ma said it wiz something tae dae way yur brother Tommy, is that true?'

'Naw, ma da said it wiz hiz ma's crazy relatives that were there last night and that a big fight happened between them awe,' Alex White, who was a year older than me and lived a couple of doors down, chipped in. There were other theories abounding as to who smashed every window in our house and why. But with the tension in my house so tight it could have bent spoons, I sure as hell wasn't about to start asking questions. Some years later however, Betty told me what had happened.

Cousin Sandra had been at a party in Springburn the night before. She had taken my sister Joan with her despite Joan being only fifteen. Afterwards Joan said that Sandra had been arguing with one of the Springburn girls, the girlfriend of Sammy Divers, the leader of the gang. Joan also said that this girl had been showing off her brand new fur coat that Sammy had bought for her and all the girls were jealous to bursting. Apparently, Sandra watched the girl put her coat into one of the bedrooms before going off to dance in the living room with her boyfriend. Sandra then went into the kitchen, found a big carving knife and snuck off to the bedroom with it. There she shredded the fur, yet somehow managed to keep it all connected so it just looked like strips of fur.

Not content to stop there, she re-entered the room and called out to the girl who was now sucking the face off her gang-leader boyfriend.

'Hey you ya cow, why don't yae put on yur fur coat and dae a wee fashion show for all of us.' Joan says that the whole party stopped at this point and every eye in the place was on Sandra who was standing holding the big knife, laughing really loudly. The girl shot off to the bedroom and let out a high-pitched scream. Then Sammy Divers turned to Sandra and shouted, 'You fucking mental-case what is wrang wae yae?'

Joan said that nothing else happened that night, mainly because Sandra had a bit of a reputation and was holding a knife. Everyone just let her leave the party without trouble, but obviously the leader of the gang had lost face in front of his girlfriend, his gang and anyone else who was there.

Our house took the brunt of the gang's revenge the next night. The guy who my father had caught was Sammy Divers. He didn't get handed over to the police. Instead, my father took matters into his own hands which meant he escorted (dragged probably) the young man home to his parents' house. Hearing about the destruction to my parents' home, not to mention that there were young children in the house, they immediately made an offer to pay to have all of our windows repaired within two days. His parents were furious and my father felt that they would deal with their son in their own way.

Two other gang members, caught by my family at the end of our street that night, were released from hospital the following morning with minor injuries. These two men had run into an alleyway, not thinking anyone would come out of the house they had just attacked, probably assuming that the people inside would have been too shocked and scared to do anything about it. How wrong you can be. Mother and Aunt Sadie took on one each. Apparently Betty and Joe had to stop Sadie from breaking her guy's neck as she was trying to pull his head off with her bare hands.

Mother, on the other hand had stuck with what she knew and punched the other one to the ground. When he didn't fight back, she left him there to go and help my dad and Abby. They were trying to get hold of the gang leader who was coming at them with a knife keeping them at bay. Apparently Lizzy just walked towards Sammy Divers not fearing the knife and head-butted him. He was knocked to the ground presumably in total shock and disbelief.

I don't recall the details of what happened to Sandra as a result of this episode, but I do know that she left our house never to live there again. I remember going with my mother to a house in the Gorbals not long after it all happened. It was the house belonging to Kate Lyons, Sandra's grandmother. There were some raised voices, but the upshot of the visit was that Sandra was to go back to the Gorbals for her own protection. She would no longer be safe walking the streets of Springburn. But also, I think, Sandra was becoming too much for my mother to handle, along with everything else. I had been just three when Sandra had first come to live with us in 1965, so she was like a big sister to me, funny, generous and always ready to protect us if we needed it. I felt her absence very deeply.

My family was like a gang, you see, and despite living in this ultra-violent world I felt safe. But I was wrong.

I must have been six when an older boy, in his late teens perhaps, from a few doors down lifted me over the garden fence. There was a motorbike covered with a tarpaulin next to the back wall of his house, and he took me underneath it. 'This won't hurt,' he said. Afterwards he gave me a two bob bit and said, 'This is our secret.' It happened a lot after that.

I can't recall being penetrated. I can remember the smell and the sound of the tarpaulin moving, but I had a sensation like fainting in the midst of something bad happening. It was as if I had separated from the rest of the world. Sometimes it even felt as if I left my body in order to escape what was being done to it.

But it wasn't only this older boy. Around the same time – I think I was still six – I was sexually abused by an older man in our street. A relative of a neighbouring family, he would visit them often. He encouraged young children to sit on his knee and he would say funny things to you and put money in your hands and cuddle you close to him. He would make you put your hand into his pocket for money and there was no lining to the pocket and you found his penis was erect. I can always remember that he would say, 'Shhhuuussshhh, you canny tell anybody aboot this, it's a secret.'

On one occasion he took me to the back of the building where his family lived and proceeded to rape me. This was in the middle of the day when our street was busy and I don't know how no one noticed what was happening. I honestly cannot remember what this experience felt like. I think that either my child's mind just simply closed out the whole thing or I went into a kind of daydream. Nothing now comes back to me about the actual sexual act that was performed on me. I have spent years in meditation classes and practised and taught self-awareness for more than twenty years, but that moment is not there for some reason. I do believe that when we are young we have natural reactions in our minds that combat such intrusions. Either way, I feel that whatever happened did not damage me mentally or emotionally. He didn't touch my soul and as I moved through life I never allowed myself to become a victim of his inappropriate act.

That sensation of being in the in-between place would begin to return from time to time, usually when bad things were happening, but sometimes just at night. I'd wake up suddenly. I might see my brothers lying there fast asleep but hear garbled voices in the darkness. Sometimes I saw the outline of a figure at the foot of my bed.

Things would happen during the day too. I'd have a premonition or find that I knew what people were thinking. I used to dread hearing a sound like a hive of bees coming from somewhere in the region of my stomach. I knew this buzzing meant I was about to be pulled through into another dimension. I was a naturally dreamy child, but it seemed to make my mother impatient if, for example, she caught me staring up at the ceiling. Usually she'd grab me by the scruff of the neck and throw me out into the street, telling me to go and play with the other kids. I'm sure she really worried I was a bit special – or, as she would have put it, that I was 'dead daft'.

And it was fear – violence or the perpetual threat of violence – that came round again and again and pushed me further and further. When it grew to such a pitch of fear that it seemed impossible to go beyond it, something popped and I knew I had gone beyond fear and into another realm. Suddenly, I was in the in-between place where I was safe because I didn't really exist. Then equally suddenly, I was back in the real world again.

4

Sickness, Spirits And Stephen

By this time my family had moved out of the one-roomed apartment in Portugal Street that had been my grandmother's to a new development. Easterhouse had been developed to relieve the overcrowding in places like the Gorbals, but it wasn't long before it became just as notorious.

Compared to the flat in Portugal Street, the apartment in Easterhouse must have seemed like a palace. It was big, clean and light with an indoor toilet and hot and cold running water. And right on the doorstep were acres of countryside for exploring. However, the move to Easterhouse wasn't a cause for rejoicing for everyone. Lizzy's brothers Michael, who was then eighteen and John, who was several years older, were distraught at my parents' departure and begged them not to leave. Lizzy had treated her younger brothers like her own sons for so many years, but now she had to let them learn to become independent of her. Betty says that for the first year or so after the move, Lizzy suffered from depression and though she tried to hide her feelings, she would well up with tears when there was talk of how Michael and John were doing.

Hiding things away seems to have been a trait of my family back then. But as my brother would find out, you needed to be sure that the things you are trying to keep secret, wouldn't be the things that actually give you away. Tommy's mischievous ways were endless in Easterhouse. He seemed to go from one little con to another. Of course he got away with most things because they were never really big scale and so mum and dad were never really any the wiser as to his behaviour. But one of his madcap attempts at petty crime did get my mother into a real flap.

Tommy had been accused of stealing pigeons from a neighbour's boy he'd gotten friendly with. His friend's mother had rounded on Lizzy, who had punched her to the ground on our landing while holding me, just a baby, in one arm. As I've already mentioned, this was my first family fight. It was over in a flash and Tommy couldn't believe his luck. He thought my mother had believed him when he said had hadn't done anything. His friend's mother went away quietly and he thought that was that.

My mother was many things, but she wasn't stupid. She had an idea that Tommy must have done something, but her law was that no one ever got near her family or had any right to punish them. Only *she* could do that. So after the other woman had left, she swiftly grabbed Tommy round the shoulders. 'Right you, don't lie tae me, huv you goat something that belongs tae that boy?' In the heat of the moment my mother hadn't heard what the woman was saying Tommy had stolen from her son.

'Ma, a swear on the Bible, ah never took anything fae that hoos, honestly Ma, ah mean it, ma hand tae God.' Lizzy surveyed a boyish face that had the look of perfect innocence. His big blue eyes so open and defenceless.

'Ok, but if I find oot that you did steal anything ma boy, you'll get what she goat only wurse.'

Tommy had of course stolen the boy's prize birds from his pigeon loft the night before. He'd stuffed them up his jumper, several at a time, then gone back for more until he'd emptied the joint. Obviously the boy had been frantic when he found out. They must have been his pride and joy. Meanwhile the birds were put in boxes with breathing holes and hidden under Tommy's bed. He was planning to build his own pigeon loft in the attic above our top floor flat. He might have been successful only he didn't realize the noise a small flock of pigeons could make when hungry and how that noise would amplify in the early hours of the morning in a small flat. It was really only a matter of time before my parents realized that their son's bedroom was turning into a scene from Alfred Hitchcock's, *The Birds*.

Tommy laughs when he tells us what happened that night.

'Sammy, can you hear a funny noise?' Both my parents had woken together with this monotonous recurring sound that seemed to be coming from the room next door.

'Coo, coo, coo, coo, coo, coo . . .' It seemed to get louder, like a choir gradually increasing in volume. 'Coo, coo, coo, coo, coo, coo . . .' Tommy was trying to feed the birds one at a time but the introduction of food excited them and in seconds a noisy feeding frenzy ensued. 'COO, COO, COO, COO!'

'Ah think it's . . . birds?' my father said with disbelief in his voice at first, but the more he listened he became certain of what he was hearing. 'It's definitely birds. Maybe they're on the roof or in the attic, Lizzy?' But even as he said this, mother was out of bed and heading for my brother's bedroom at speed.

'What the fuck is this? Sammy come in here quick,' she shouted loudly after bursting into the next room to find Tommy holding two of the birds, desperately trying to shush them. Lizzy started to wave her arms about in the air and scream. 'Arrhhhh . . . get tae fuck ya dirty, flea-infested bastards. Gon, get oooot ae ma hoos.' I don't believe that any birds took offence at these allegations, but in the uproar Tommy knocked over some more boxes, letting more panic-filled birds out into the room.

By the time my father arrived in the doorway there were feathers everywhere and the noise of frantic pigeons flying around Lizzy's head and waving hands. My dad came to the rescue once again. He opened the window as wide as it would go and slowly began to direct the birds out of the room in as calm a way as he knew how, bringing an end to my mother's Tippi Hedren impersonation. But mother wasn't for becoming calm just yet . . .

'What the fuck are you doing with those manky things in my hoos? Did you steal them from that wee boy, ya dirty wee lying thieving bastard, I'll . . .' Lizzy was now in full flight herself, slapping Tommy who was now under the bed covers.

'Mammy, I never stole them, they just came to me because I put bread on the windy cill, ah swear, that's what happened, honestly.'

There was a lot more flapping and a couple more smacks, but being homing pigeons the birds managed to get back to their loft safely and unharmed. Tommy's daft plan had been to re-train them to come back to him. He would then sell them to people, with the hope that the pigeons would keep returning to him so he could sell them on again to other buyers.

The last year of the sixties was one that really stands out for me. The first reason for this was because I ended up in hospital for two months, having contracted rheumatic fever just before my seventh birthday. My one strong memory of first feeling ill was that I was out playing with other children when all of a sudden I fell down in the street and couldn't walk. I remember that the other children thought I was mucking around and began to laugh at me. One of my friends, Alex White, kicked me and told me to get up. I say friend . . .

I don't even remember getting back to my house that day. I'm told that my father came running out into the street and lifted me in his arms and carried me home, where I remained unconscious until the doctor came. The doctor immediately called for an ambulance to take me to Stobhill Hospital, which was close by. My memory of this time is a bit hazy, because of how ill I was.

Several children in the ward, the Edward Unit, had the same illness and while I was there, one boy died. My parents were frightened. Lizzy had already lost one child and she really thought there was a chance I would die too.

The hospital was within walking distance from where we lived, which meant I had many visitors. 'Did you say it was rheumatic fever you had Gordon, or wiz it dramatic fever, ha-ha-ha?' My brother Jonny teased me in front of the small group of people who were sitting around my bed, now laughing loudly.

My cousin Sandra was a regular visitor too. She brought things from the joke shop. The first thing that all the kids in the ward loved was a whoopee cushion, which she put under a cloth on the seat next to my bed before inviting different visitors to take a seat. The other favourite was fake dog pooh which she left on the floor near the nurse's station, causing the ward sister to fly off the handle at some orderly.

I was in that ward for two months and pumped full of antibiotics. What should've seemed like a long time to a child of seven felt like a mere moment. Yet I can recall the feeling that of being sad to be separated from my mad, uproarious family. I know I cried when my parents left me after evening visits ended. One time I even tried to escape, but got caught twenty minutes later in the hospital kitchen, because I had stopped to steal sponge cake and custard. The lady who caught me – I think she was a domestic in the ward – sat with me and read to me from a children's book until I fell asleep.

When I eventually returned to my family the house at first seemed empty. I was to be kept at home to convalesce for a while. As the others were at school or work, it was only me and my mum at home. She would bring me milk and biscuits around eleven o'clock each morning when she stopped to have a break from cleaning and washing clothes. I have happy memories of this time and a strong sense of being loved and nurtured by my mother with no one else around. The rest of the family also treated me differently for a while after I first came out of hospital and it made me feel like I was special.

One day, not long after I was home from hospital, my mother told me to go out into the front garden. It was a nice day and she thought the fresh air and sunshine would help give me strength. There was nothing particularly different about this day until I became aware of a feeling in my stomach, a tugging sensation that was sort of pulling me out of our garden and making me stand on the pavement in front of our low hedge. I can still see this now in my mind as I write. It really is my purest memory.

Mansel Street looked longer than usual, maybe because of the complete absence of people. There were normally lots of children playing and adults getting off buses at the far corner, which was where I was now compelled to look. I distinctly remember a figure standing there at the end of the empty street. He began to move towards me. It was Ummy, a friend of my parents.

No one can remember how or why he got that nickname, but it was all we ever knew him as. Ummy was a man of that time, a nice man. I found out later that he was originally from Poland and now worked as a tic tac man at the races and lived in a hostel. I also found out he'd been my grandmother Sarah's boyfriend after Bernhard her dandified, street-fighting husband had left her.

When Ummy visited our house it was usually after he had been to the racetracks and won big. Then he brought money and gifts for my mother and for us. He used to give all the kids in our street a big brown penny too. Kids used to queue up when they saw him come off the number four bus and some would even mob him. They might have to laugh at his little ditties and corny jokes until they got their reward. But this day it was only Ummy and me.

I felt like he was really happy. He smiled at me and that made me smile. Ummy had the exact same smile as my Auntie Sadie. I didn't know it then, but he was her father and also my Uncle Michael's. The other thing that stood out in my memory about this moment was the ditty he was singing. It made no sense at all, but the words stuck in my head and are still as clear today. 'We will be buried in Dalbeth, we will be buried in Dalbeth . . .' Over and over he sang these words until I began to sing with him. But when I began to mimic his words, he began to retreat back up to the end of the street, gliding backwards just as quickly as he had come towards me. I wanted to go with him. I mean I really wanted to run to get to him, but my feet were stuck to the pavement. Ummy was waving in the distance and I heard him calling goodbye, which was the last thing that happened before he was gone and I could move again.

Still singing, I turned and ran into the house where my mother was standing at the kitchen sink peeling potatoes. I grabbed her skirt impatiently and blurted out, 'Ummy, Ummy was here!' My mother spun on the spot and her eyes seemed to burn through me, but she didn't speak. Her mouth just sort of opened. Then these words came out of me: 'We will be buried in Dalbeth, we will be buried in Dalbeth.'

'Stop that!' My mother looked scared in a way I had never seen before and I remember that the happy feeling I'd drawn from Ummy was now fast leaving me.

'He was singing that song Mammy, "We will be buried in Dalbeth".'

'Get oot oh here right noo and stop telling lies, yae didny see Ummy, go on get oot right now.' Her open hand smacked me around the top of the legs.

I felt dejected and scared. I had no idea why my mother was scolding me like this when all I had done was bring her the happy news that her friend was outside on the path and was singing a happy song. I didn't go out front, instead I went into the back garden and played with a ball. I can't remember anything else being said about what happened in the kitchen that day.

Many years later I asked my mother about Ummy and she told me that he'd died in an accident. He'd been found unconscious at the number four bus terminus and died several days later in hospital from his injuries. The backs of the buses were open then and no one knew if he fell off or was pushed. Ummy had no family to pay for a funeral, so my parents helped to bury him with what little money they had at the time. My mother was quite embarrassed to speak about it because all they could afford was what was known then as a 'pauper's grave' – in Dalbeth Cemetery in the east end of Glasgow.

Ummy had been buried a week when I saw him in the street. That's why my mother freaked out. She told me that no one but a few of her family from the Gorbals knew about the grave. It wasn't something that would have ever been discussed when children were in earshot.

***

'Heh, wait tae yae hear this, oor Uncle Mick and Auntie Sylvia are coming to stay in oor hoos, ah heard ma ma telling ma da, but don't tell anybody that ah telt yae, oh and by the way, oor Tommy's getting merrit!' Jonny loved it when he had info to pass on to us. He was good at listening in at the living room door when my parents were talking quietly about things they didn't want us to know about. Normally he'd want something for his information, but I think this time he was so excited about who was coming, he let that slide.

I remember thinking, *Who ur oor Uncle Mick and Aunty Sylvia anyway?* I'd never met these people. Michael had only ever been a rare visitor. He was one of Lizzy's brothers, the ones she'd left behind in Portugal Street when the rest of the family moved to Easterhouse. Later my dad had persuaded him to join the Navy and he had gone off to sea before I was born. When he returned, he went to live in London and met Sylvia. They got married after just a few short months of courting. Before long Sylvia persuaded Michael to start his own roofing business and it turned out to be very successful.

As for Jonny's other bit of news, about Tommy getting married, the idea of it got me very excited. I had never been to a wedding before, but I had experienced something of what happened at them. In Glasgow, children gathered around the cars that were taking a wedding party off to church. As the cars drove off, the windows would get rolled down and someone inside would throw a handful of coins out at the crowd of excited kids. They would then shout, or scream, 'SCRAMBLE' diving in all directions to grab the flying pennies, thrupenny bits and tanners – if you were lucky. This thought alone made my brother's impending wedding something to look forward to. It hadn't dawned on me that I would be in one of the cars.

The day of Tommy's wedding to his wife Maureen I got to wear a suit with a waistcoat and a dickey-bow. I was so full of nervous excitement from about five o'clock that morning that I fell asleep when we got to the reception. Uncle Mick and Aunt Sylvia arrived from London very late, so I didn't get to meet them until the next morning. I remember opening the door to my parents' bedroom and seeing a woman with perfect, puffy blonde hair sitting up, very straight-backed in my parents' bed. She was reading something, I recall, and looked like a film star. 'Well hello you, you must be Gordon I imagine?' I nodded my head in the most bashful way, resting my chin on my chest. Part of me was tempted to turn and run away, but there was something about this woman that made me feel very drawn to her, so I was compelled to stay. Her voice was very different to any I had ever heard before. She was English and I honestly had never heard an English voice except on television or radio, but here was an English woman talking to me right here and now.

'Oh I hope you're not shy because I have heard that you love to tell jokes and sing songs, is that right?' Again, I couldn't speak, instead I nodded for the second time. I could feel myself blushing. 'Look, this is for you.' She had taken something from a handbag beside her on the bed. Now I saw it was a big, green pound note and I think my heart stopped right then and there. *Oh my God*. I think I may have snatched off two of her fingers as I grabbed it out of her hand.

'Jonny, Sammy, look at what av goat, it's a pound, a real pound.' I was halfway up the hall by this time, but I'm sure my voice could be heard up and down the street.

That was how I met my Aunt Sylvia. She and my uncle stayed with us for the next two days and they must have been the happiest of my young life up to this point. Sylvia was elegant and fashionable, a real lady and I was spoiled rotten by her. I couldn't stop saying her name: 'Sylvia, Sylvia, Sylvia . . .' I had never heard that name before but now I spoke about her so much that it annoyed my two brothers.

It turned out Sylvia and Michael had a son who was about my age. Sylvia said he was dying to meet me and that at Christmas they would bring me to London to meet him.

Seeing the way they liked to spoil me, my brother tried to use me to get more money out of them. 'Gordon, ask Uncle Mick if he needs anything fae the shop and he'll gee yae money fur going.' I didn't want to do that to get money out of my uncle. Besides, the pound that Sylvia had given me meant that I would be rich for years to come.

'Naw, am no gonny ask fur anything, leave me alaine and stoap being greedy.' Jonny was never one to give up that easily. He knew he could always get me to do things. He just had to bide his time: 'Ah think Auntie Sylvia wants you to brush her hair fur hur, goan ask hur if she want yae tae dae that.' He was getting desperate, but again I would have nothing to do with it. I didn't want anything from my new favourite person in the world other than to be close to her and listen to her speak.

I remember almost crying when Sylvia left our house to return to London, even though she told me that I could come and visit for Christmas. In my young mind that felt like a lifetime away, though it was only six weeks. When they left, I had the same feeling I'd had when my parents left me when I was in hospital – and Jonny must have seen this as his chance to get money out of me.

He began by telling me that I should share my pound with him because Sylvia would like me if she thought I was a kind person like her. I thought about it and I *almost* gave in because it sounded right, but something made me hang on to it. Then he started to tell me that everybody got a gift from my aunt, but she must have forgotten about him and he didn't want to ask her, because he thought that wouldn't have been right. He sounded so sincere when he said, 'It disny matter Gordon, maybe you could buy me a wee sweety or something if that's ok wae you, ah don't want much jest a wee thing, if that's ok?' His pathetic tone broke me. I wouldn't have minded, but not only did I end up giving him half of my money, but he even got me to go to the shops, change the money and bring it back to him, which I did running all the way because of how sorry I felt for him. 'Here Jonny, there's your half, diz that make yae feel better noo?'

The Christmas in London that followed was the best reward for any kindness I'd ever shown. That week was like being in heaven. My sister Joan travelled with me to London on the train, which in those days took about ten hours. Joan told me later that I talked continuously through the entire journey. I was telling our fellow passengers about my aunt and uncle and that I was going to meet my cousin Stephen for the first time, but that we had talked on the phone, and how he talked funny because he was English and then I would mimic my cousin's voice for whoever would listen. I can only imagine how annoying and embarrassing that must have been for my sister, then about sixteen.

But nothing would make me go to sleep, and when we eventually got to their house in Morden, Stephen was in the same awake, hyper state as me. We immediately ran to his toy room, which he couldn't wait to show me. I don't even think I said hello to my aunt and uncle. I hadn't ever been in a house like this. It was a large semi-detached with four big bedrooms, two living rooms, a dining room and it had a bathroom and a separate small room for the toilet.

Stephen was the only person I knew who had a room for just his toys. In his garden there was a little goal with a net and a big pond with goldfish. You could see it from the living room, through really big glass sliding doors that opened onto the garden. Stephen had bikes in the garage and I was allowed to play with one of them the next day when we woke up. I don't remember seeing the grown-ups. We got up so early and Stephen dragged me into his shed to show me his train set and then we got the bikes out – there were three and they were choppers, with handlebars that stood up high like a Harley motorbike.

This was all a bit too much for me and I remember Joan telling me to calm down whenever we were alone in the room that we were sleeping in. She could see how overwhelming it all was for me, but she was watching over me and reminded me that we were just visiting and that I wasn't to get carried away: 'Remember Gordon, you can only play wae these things, they urny yours to take home.'

She needn't have worried. Many of the toys I'd been playing with *would* come home with me because Stephen just got a whole new batch of things for Christmas – as did I. Honestly, for a boy from my background to be given so much at one time was absolutely amazing. Joan was also shocked because Aunt Sylvia had bought some pretty amazing things for her too. I remember how embarrassed Joan looked when we exchanged presents and she saw the little tokens that were all my mother could afford to send to Sylvia, Michael and Stephen.

But once again, my sister needn't have felt embarrassed. Sylvia was one of the most generous and gracious people I have ever met. With every fibre of her being she made people feel comfortable, no matter who and no matter what their situation. She was one of the greatest people to touch my life and the teachings she passed on to me have remained deep in my heart along with all my most precious memories of her.

Sylvia may have been elegant, but that didn't mean she was cold and formal. She was soft, cuddly and affectionate and would ask me how I felt – which was totally new to me. She was mummyish, and where once I had been clenched and fearful of rows and violence, I now began to relax. Sylvia taught me how to be a child, to play. Of course, I'd played football in the street with boys in Glasgow – and I had my friend Alex White next door – but now for the first time, I had a friend I could play games of the imagination with, talk to about things and ask personal questions.

Sylvia gave me the greatest Christmas a little boy like me could have imagined and I know that she got even more out of it than I did. Anyone could look at her and see that happiness was oozing out of her every expression. I had no idea at the time, but she told me later that she just felt something in her heart that said I would help her in a way that no monetary reward could ever equal. What a strange thing for an adult to feel when they look at a little seven-year-old boy.

5

Singing Siblings And Seventies Fashion

Hogmanay is party time in Scotland, or at least it was when I was growing up. My mother would cook a big steak pie and homemade vegetable soup. The kitchen would smell good for the entire day.

It was the one night of the year when the children were allowed to stay up till after midnight. Just before midnight arrived, when the bells from Stobhill Hospital down the road rang out, Lizzy would fill our table with shortbread, Madeira cake, sandwiches, crisps and bottles of pop. My father would line up beers and any other alcoholic drinks on the bar. Remember we had a fancy one with leatherette and studs.

In Scotland, the New Year had more emphasis put on it than Christmas. Well, that's if you hadn't been in London for Christmas. I'd just returned with toys, money and all sorts of goodies that made me the envy of every child in our street. 'Gordon, did you really get tae go a chopper bike?', 'Has your cousin got three bikes or iz it four?', 'Ur your uncle and auntie pure, dead rich?', 'How big is their hoos?' Questions like these and more, many, many more were being asked of me when I returned to Mansel Street and as I remember, made me feel like the most special child in the whole of Scotland.

There was such an excitement in the air and not just around me. It wasn't just any old New Year, as we were moving into a whole new decade. I believe people actually thought that something would appear in the sky at the stroke of midnight to mark the occasion. People just kept turning up at our house – neighbours, plus family and friends – and for the first time I could remember, we had a party without a fight. (Some would say it couldn't have been a proper party without a fight.)

It was a night of dancing and singing – and in our family that meant something. There were lots of good singers in our house, so people took it seriously. There was a kind of unspoken order of appearance based on talent. Considered high up on the bill were my Uncle John, his wife Cathy and her brother Peter if he was visiting. And most definitely my mother and Betty were right up there.

Usually, others were encouraged to sing first as a kind of warm up act – that might include neighbours or children or strangers who had wandered in off the street. 'Ok, howz aboot that wee wumin way the broon dress giving us a wee song, howz about it, hen?' There was a real element of showbiz at these parties, especially once the star performers got going. Betty would sing one of her favourites like 'Will You Still Love Me Tomorrow' but that night Lizzy brought the house down when she belted out Stevie Wonder's 'For Once in My Life' with full dramatic outstretched arms to finish. That was it. No one wanted to follow her. The curtain dropped to thunderous applause.

'That was brilliant Lizzy, geez another wan,' my Uncle John begged. He wanted the singing to go on all night.

'Naw John, a better heat those sausage rolls noo.' Lizzy sheepishly moved out to the kitchen as though she regretted what she had just done, but I'm sure inside she loved it.

There was certainly a different kind of buzz building in the air as we said goodbye to the swinging sixties and hello to the sensational seventies. I can only assume the God of Fashion got drunk and passed out for several years. In our family photos from the early seventies we all looked like gypsies, unkempt and scruffy with lots of messy curly hair. I can still hear my mother shouting at Betty and Joan for wearing big, clumpy platform boots: 'Those things are fucking death traps. You'll fall and break your neck wearing them, or at least your ankle, you mark my words lassie.' Of course every young woman was wearing platforms, and most of the men. And where there were platforms, there had to be flairs.

Sammy was beginning to discover fashion in the early seventies. He was going on thirteen, that horrible age for boys when they are not sure if they are still a child or a young adult. It's when they get awkward and bashful around the older members of their family and ratty or downright bad-tempered with the younger ones.

Jonny was a little devil then. He would tell anyone he could find to come and spy on Sammy as he got dressed to go out with his mates to a 'record session'. This was a kind of early disco held in community centres or in local school halls. They were set up for young teenagers to go and listen to pop music, dance, get to know one another and drink soft drinks. Or if it was near us it was more likely to be greasy, spotty teenagers, smoking, under-age drinking and – obviously – fighting.

Jonny loved to wind Sammy up about his attempts to look cool, as was the duty of an annoying younger brother then. 'Ma, Jonny's outside wae eez pals and they're laughing at me, tell him tae beat it or I'll run oot there and batter the lot owe them.' Sammy had noticed that his two younger brothers and pals had gathered outside his bedroom window at the back of the house to spy on him as he tried to brush the waves out of his dark blonde hair to make it look longer.

Lizzy was getting on with something in the kitchen, washing up dishes or wiping down surfaces at the time, creating that bleached smell we had all come to know and love so much. 'Just ignore him then and hurry up and get oot, awe yur pals are standing in oor path so hurry up and don't bother wae him.'

'Bit Ma, he's outside the windy and he's making faces and laughing noo, that's it am gonny kill um.'

Jonny was making faces through the window, squashing his face flat against the pane and then acting up for all his friends to see and hear: 'Check big Sammy the poof, brushing hes hair like a wumin. Look at eez face, eez getting dead annoyed.'

Seconds later, Sammy was out of the house like a flash and rolling around the back garden with Jonny having a right old scrap. 'Poof, ya wee shite, I'll gee yae poof.' Slaps and punches flew from both brothers as they wrestled on the ground before Lizzy arrived to pull them apart. 'Bastards, the pair oh yae are driving me fucking daft wae awe this fighting, noo fucking stoap it!' Lizzy was furious at being pulled away from her cleaning once again. 'My nerves are shattered wae you boyz. Jonny, Gordon, get in! Sammy, get oot!!! And they rest awe you lot, fuck off back tae where yae come fae.'

So it was back to reality with a bang for me. My London high life seemed a far distant memory at times like this. I was reminded of where I really came from. Violence was always in the air. I'd get cuffed, smacked, feel the back of Lizzie's hand, get beaten up by my brothers. Everyone in that confined space suffered from rage, and the smallest thing could set it off. Fighting was the only way my family knew to sort out disagreements and my mother had the shortest fuse of all, and when she was angry she was really frightening.

I hated it. My stomach used to turn. Oh God, no! Please don't start, please don't fight. I'd go cold with fear, freeze and try to retreat inside myself. I couldn't think straight. If I was playing outside and the shouting started I didn't want to go in. I'd sit outside the front door on the pavement. Often I used to hide in the shed or under a bush, my legs trembling. Sometimes if we kids were inside, we'd run outside, even if it was night and we were in the house in vest and pants. Home became a living hell in those times. In the mornings I prayed that people would be talking to each other and it wasn't going to kick off all over again. I wanted everything to be okay. I never wound my mother up like my brothers and sisters. I was too afraid. I would have done *anything* to make it all alright.

But it wouldn't be alright. Until the next school holidays. At Sylvia and Mike's I had entered a very different, magical world. There was always a roast joint with crackling on Sundays and the house was filled with the beautiful, transporting smell of Estée Lauder. Stephen and I would put on shows and do impersonations of famous characters on the TV. I did Kenneth Williams and Stephen would do Frank Spencer. His party piece was 'Puppy Love' by Donny Osmond and mine was Michael Jackson's 'Ben'. On Saturdays Michael drove us to see Crystal Palace and I marvelled at the wonderful fantasy football of George Best and Rodney Marsh. And so, although I was ready to go back home at the end of the holidays, I'd found a new form of happiness. In these gentle, nurturing surroundings I was beginning to open up.

***

I can honestly say that as young as seven, I could *feel* emotional exchanges between people around me like a physical force. If these exchanges were hostile, they would affect me worse than a physical slap. Once I even had to go to hospital to have my knee x-rayed. It turned out that my father had arthritis in his knee and that I was feeling his pain.

But it was around Easter time 1970 that I first became conscious of death. (I still didn't know that Ummy was dead, to me he was very much alive.) My parents had taken Sammy, Jonny and me to London over the Easter school break to spend time with Stephen. Now I got to show my brothers all the fab things I had played with at Christmas. But a strange thing happened to me when we were on the train coming home. If I close my eyes I can still see the dimly lit carriage, with a big sliding door separating us from the rest of the train. My parents sat facing each other, mother was smoking periodically and Sammy was sprawled over the long seat beside dad. He was drawing on pages of a notepad he had bought in the station. Jonny, on the other side of Lizzy from me, was shuffling a deck of playing cards he had bought, probably trying to work out ways to cheat people. It might have been the sound and motion of the train, or the speed at which objects outside in the semi-darkness were flashing past quickly and hypnotically, but my mind went into a kind of buzz that I now recognize as an altered state of conscious-ness, a sort of trance. I remember being in two places at the same time and that both were as real as each other. I knew I was on a train with my family because I could see them and hear them, but in a way I wasn't really connected to them. My mind was somewhere else, in a place that I recog-nized. I was in the house of my friend Alex White in Mansel Street, standing beside his mother's bed.

This experience was so real that I knew if I reached out my hands and touched Mrs White, I would have felt her; that she was as real to me as the people beside me in the train compartment. I then saw Alex. His father was holding him and telling him that his mother had gone to heaven. I remember Alex was holding a large Easter egg in his hands. It was covered with bright shinny wrapping paper and in a box that covered the top and bottom only. He was crying, but then he was silent and I felt his sadness because it was in me as well. I wanted it to go away. I had to fight not to cry in front of my family now. The rest of the memory is quite unclear, but I know I dropped into a sleep and when I woke it was morning and I was in my house in Mansel Street.

The first thing I wanted to do was go and find Alex White. I knew that something sad had happened and I knew, too, that I had to be with him. But before I could leave our house my mother took hold of my arm and spoke to me.

'Ah don't want you going near Alex White's hoos today. Do yae hear me noo?' I heard her very well and though her voice wasn't raised, there was enough warning in it to keep me from going to Alex's house to look for him. 'They poor people have had bad news, so stay away, ok!' I got the message, but I already knew the bad news the White family had received. I already knew that Alex's mother had died.

I don't recall exactly how many days passed before I got to be with Alex, but it wasn't that many. Death was more a part of people's lives back then. It often occurred in homes rather than hospitals. I remember being in my friend's house and that the furniture there was being moved around from one room to the next. They were freeing up the larger room that his mother had passed in so that they could bring in beds for Alex and his brother George. Life really did go on, grief or no grief, and the living took pride of place over the dead.

For children our age, death was more present but it wasn't spoken about. We followed the example of our parents and kept quiet about the bigger questions of life. But there is a magic that all children have, especially when things are hidden from them. It's a childlike telepathy so that without ever having to say anything, there's an understanding. That is what I remember sharing with my friend. I took him my own chocolate Easter egg which I brought back from London to show off to all my friends in our street because it was so big. I knew that he wasn't ever going to open his own egg, as it was the last thing his mother had bought for him. I honestly don't know how I knew all of this, but I did. It was still all inside me from the experience I had had on the train, though I didn't ever tell my friend this. I was moved to share my own chocolate and when I did he told me what I already knew: 'I'm never, ever gonny eat my Easter egg because ma mammy bought it fur me, so I've put it in the display cabinet in the living room so I can remember her when I look at it.'

There isn't much you can offer someone to help them after they experience the death of a loved one, but something sat well in me, that my small gesture was the right thing in that moment. We played for a while with toy cars in his new bedroom as people lifted mattresses and chest of drawer sets over our heads. They were getting it ready for whatever would come next.

Our own house was also being rearranged at the same time in preparation for a new arrival at 97 Mansel Street. Due to ill health, my grandad Bernhard was coming to stay with us. Just when our house was beginning to feel spacious – my two brothers and me had a single bed each in the biggest of our three bedrooms, and Joan had been enjoying having the middle room to herself – things changed again.

My grandfather looked old at seventy and he seemed quite infirm, oh, and half deaf. The moment he arrived the volume in everyone's voices seemed to go up by several decibels. 'Why don't you sit in this chair?' My father motioned the older man to sit on the chair normally reserved for himself, but grandad just stood looking at him blankly. 'SIT DOON HERE!' my dad shouted. It must have felt strange and awkward for the old man who had never known us as his family to now have to come and live with us.

'Maybe he canny talk, dae yae think so?' I asked. Sammy just looked uncomfortable and shy like he wanted to get out and away.

'Jeest stop looking right at him ya wee pest and stop talking aboot him he might be kidding on he canny hear yae,' Sammy said in a whispered tone. Then Jonny who had been observing his grandfather with great scrutiny spoke softly in his direction: 'Eh, dae yae want me tae hing yur coat up fur yae grandda?' It was clear that Jonny was looking at the bulging top pocket of the old man's overcoat that he wouldn't take off. Jonny extended his hand in grandad's direction.

'GET TAE FUCK!!! Ah know what yur up tae.' The volume of the old man's voice made the whole house shake and my two brothers and me jumped with pure fright. This frail-looking old man could roar like his daughter and what he missed in hearing, he surely made up for in awareness, no doubt from many years of being streetwise.

My grandfather's stay in our house was up and down.

Sometimes Lizzy would have to be kind in the way she spoke to him, especially when the old man looked weak and frail, but after several months of being rested in our middle room, where he just seemed to sit up in bed for most of his time, reading books or checking the racing form in the daily newspaper, he began to regain strength, and this is when the battles between him and my mother began.

'Lizzy that soup is cold,' he would shout from my father's chair, where he was now taking his meals.

'What? Ya ungrateful auld bastard, yae weren't saying that when yae were staying in whorehouses in the Gorbals, there fuck awae wrong wae the soup, noo eat it and shut it.' Of course, their voices were even more than usually raised because of grandad's hearing problem. It took me a while to understand that deaf people always spoke louder than those they were talking to. Grandad had no idea how loud he was, but he wasn't going to risk not being heard. Again, I became aware that unlike the rest of my family, I would shake nervously when these verbal battles would happen.

'People always said that you were like my mother Lizzy, but they were wrong, my mother had compassion, you are just a bitter cow, so shove your soup.'

She did – down the sink.

Grandad was beginning to recover from what was a very bad case of bronchitis, made worse by lungs damaged from years of smoking. When he dressed to go out for the day, we all noticed that he looked smart. He demanded that his shirt be pressed to look like new. He still wore silk ties and neck scarves under some pretty fly looking woollen overcoats. When he went out he was the image of a very well-turned-out gentleman.

We never learned much about these days out, but his return

always excited us because he brought us sweets and silver sixpences when he cashed his weekly pension.

He wasn't the kind of grandfather who told stories of his past. In fact he was very secretive if you asked him about where he grew up or about his own family.

'Grandda, huv you goat brothers and sister and wits their names?' I would ask him, only to get a lesson in how to speak.

'Try not to speak like that son, say, HAVE YOU GOT BROTHERS . . .' But I liked talking to him, because I could blether away and much of the time he didn't hear me. Sometimes he would laugh or shake his head and smile at me in response to my gibberish.

Jonny asked him how to put on a line at the bookies and somewhat reluctantly grandad showed him. He went so far as to teach him how to read form of horses and jockeys.

My dad liked to talk to grandad about the Gorbals and the notorious people there. We loved these conversations. They couldn't talk in whispers so we could all hear about it from wherever we were in the house. I vaguely remember hearing about one of our relatives who tried to rob a bank, while another was said to be the worst safe-blower in Glasgow and blasted himself out of a window.

Only Lizzy found him difficult. As I say, she was angry with him from time to time, but I never saw her confront him directly about leaving her mother and her brothers and sister when they were young. For all she raged at her father, it was plain to see that there was always a part of her that cared for him. She was looking after him in her home, after all, feeding him and washing and pressing his clothes. No matter what dreadful things he had done in the past. She was like him in looks and I'm sure in temperament too. If he gave us a stern look, we took it seriously, but most of the time he would smile softly with eyes almost identical to our mother's.

He was the only grandparent that Sammy, Jonny and I had known. Sarah and my father's parents, had all died before we were born. So my grandad holds a bit of a special place in my heart, especially when I think back to Monday mornings at school playtime, when he would appear in one of his great looking gangster-like coats at the school gates and smile as he passed a shilling to Sammy, as he was the oldest, and sixpence each to Jonny and me. Again, it was a soft smile that made his eyes look like they were laughing that stands out the most in my memory of my grandad.

His eldest son Barney, also came into my life that same year. Lots of my mother's relatives turned up to see my grandad. If he had been absent from most of his family's lives for a long time, now he was living with us, he was like a fairground attraction.

But when Uncle Barney came to visit it turned out he also had some bad news. He had lung cancer and had been given six months to live.

I remember that my mother looked like a truck had hit her. I believe that Lizzy felt that she could always protect all her family – or that she would die trying. But when cancer was the threat, it was out of her hands and she was rendered helpless, a state she didn't know how to accept very well. Barney was her elder brother and she adored him the same way she did her other siblings.

Once she had been arrested in the Gorbals. The police had been putting handcuffs on Barney and they had started kicking and punching him while his hands were behind his back. My uncle was cheeky and sarcastic and had no love for the police, like most people from the Gorbals. He had been shouting and causing a disturbance in the street. He was drunk because his first wife, Jean Cooper, had died with their baby in childbirth. In fact, he had been drinking for days and was out of control when the police stopped him and cautioned him. Barney couldn't remember much of what happened next, except that he was at the receiving end of a beating from the police, when his young sister and her husband came running towards him. He watched as Lizzy took the constable by the lapels and head-butted him – a Gorbal's Kiss, as it was known. Barney was let go with a caution hours later for disturbing the peace, but Lizzy was charged with assault and fined.

She was his protector and he had come to her when he had gotten the news of his illness. I think he needed her strength. He came straight from north London where he lived with his wife and four kids just to be with Lizzy. He was older than her by two years, but she was like his mother and though, of course, he knew she couldn't fix him this time, he wanted to be around her and my father.

They had helped my uncle on many occasions when he'd needed a lawyer, for example, or when he had found himself in trouble with women. Like his father he was a rogue, but a loveable rogue nonetheless. Like his sister he was very tough, but also very generous and caring. He tried to appear hard, but Uncle Barney had a real twinkle in his eye like his father's and a great sense of humour. In time he found a way to make light of his very serious illness and learned to handle it. His words from all that time ago have stayed with me. At the time, I didn't know why they would have such relevance and meaning in my life, but I know that my body shuddered as if I had just had an electric shock: 'Lizzy, I'm gonny die

6

Births, Deaths, Marriages

In the early seventies, Betty moved into a rented flat just around the corner from us. Her children, Stephen and Michelle, became an extension of our family and practically lived with us for the first few years of their lives. Either she and the kids were in our house, or we would be visiting them in her tiny place. Lizzy just shook her head when asked how it felt to be a granny again. 'More fucking mouths to feed, ah jest wish they would go and huv a life before huvin fuckin' waens.'

Stephen and Michelle seemed to be contented, easy going kids. I'm sure that was partly because their mother was much more tactile and openly affectionate than Lizzy ever was. 'Put that fucking baby doon,' she'd say. 'You are gonny spoil it. Waens shoodny be lifted up every two minutes Betty!'

Lizzy was never particularly comfortable picking up her grandchildren or playing games with them. She seemed too busy, cooking, cleaning and getting on with the general running of a house filled with people to have time to amuse them. Yet everything she did was for the children in her life.

I began travelling to London on every school holiday. My aunt and uncle loved to have me there to be with Stephen. A boisterous child and obviously very spoiled, he didn't have many friends of his own age around him. He hated it when I had to return to my family.

For me, life just kept getting better and better. I was taken on holidays with my cousin in the summer break. We went to Brighton, Margate and Studland Bay. Apart from London, I hadn't been outside Glasgow. I don't think I had seen the sea or a beach, let alone theme parks like Dreamland in Margate or Chessington Zoo. I was treated to clothes and toys that my brothers would never get, not to mention a trip to a Berni Inn where I tasted my first sirloin steak. It was all so amazing for a little boy who came from a struggling working class family in Glasgow to be taken to so many places and treated like this.

Then during the summer holidays of 1971 Stephen asked me if I had ever been to the Bahamas. Now, let me think, had I been to the . . . shut the front door! I had never even heard of the Bahamas let alone been there. It turned out Aunt Sylvia's brother lived out there with his wife and three children, and they wanted to fly Stephen and his mother out for a holiday. I was to ask my parents if I could be allowed to accompany them. Wow, wow and again, wow. I remember how excited I was while my uncle was talking on the phone to my mother. I was jumping up and down at his side watching him smiling broadly.

'Gordon is beside me and he wants to ask you something, Lizzy.' Michael then handed the phone to me, which I snatched without thinking and just garbled my words out at high speed down the mouthpiece in the most excited high-pitched tone: 'Mammy, Mammy, I'm no kidding, Sylvia wants me to go on an aeroplane and go tae America and then go tae the Bahaman Islands and there's sea and it's near where the rockets fly tae the moon, can ah go Mammy, please, can ah go, please, gonny let me, please Ma . . .?'

'Ok, but . . .'

'Ah kin go Stephen, I'm coming with yae, oh my God ma mammy said a kin go.' I hadn't even listened to anything else my mother was trying to say to me over the phone about how I should behave, I had only heard the initial, ok, and I was off. It was the best moment of my life – again – and for the rest of that trip my cousin and I talked every moment of every day about the many things we were going to do in the Bahamas.

My trip of a lifetime was several months away. Even so, I can still remember how good it felt when I got home to tell people that I was going to this amazingly exotic place with my cousin and aunt, the most important people in my now not so small world.

'You are so lucky, so yae are, ah wish ah could go tae that place your gon tae.' Charlie Bell, a boy who lived on our street who I used to play with was sitting on the low wall at the side of our path: 'We are going to Port Seaton for a holiday.' He spoke absently like he was uninterested in his own conversation.

'Where's that Charlie?' I asked him, hoping to carry on the conversation so I could talk more about my trip.

'Don't know, but it's really far ah think.' He seemed to be caught up on something else as his words sounded so distant now. With that, I knew I had to find someone else to brag to. By now Charlie was picking his nose and looking at what he found up there with more interest than anything I had to offer.

The time spent at home with my family seemed to pass so slowly and school was a bore. As much as it felt good to talk to people in Glasgow about this, it wasn't the same as talking to Stephen or my aunt about it, especially Sylvia, who had already been there and could describe some of the fantastic sights to us. Every day separated from my English relatives felt like prison. Restlessness lived inside of me and there was nothing I could do to evict it.

Christmas break couldn't come quickly enough for me and I know it was the same for my cousin. When my aunt called my mother on a Sunday night we all listened from the living room. Lizzy took the call in the hall at our new posh phone table made of wrought iron with yellow leatherette padded seat. We could always tell when it was Sylvia she was talking to because of the way she spoke: 'Hello, five, eight, one, three, who is calling please? Oh it's you Sylvia, I wasn't expecting it to be you, near I wiz.' She knew fine well who was about to call. 'Tell me now, howz everything wae you and oor Michael then? Oh that's lovely so it iz, oh that's fabulous so it iz . . .' and on it went. It was funny when she dropped a clanger, as we called it and let some of her natural dialect slip through. 'Aht's gud yeez ur awe keepin' well, isnay?'

As far back as I can remember, I don't think my mother ever put on a phone voice for another living soul. Jonny would often be in the living room mimicking her. 'Oh iz that right Sylvia, yes Sylvia, three bags fucking full Sylvia, if you say so Sylvia.' My mother would start to get wound up, 'Hold on a wee minute, Sylvia I just need to talk tae wan awe ar boyz, hold on please wid yae?' Her hand would tightly cover the mouthpiece as she spun her head towards the living room. 'Ya wee bastard Jonny, when ah get oaf this fucking phone I'll break your skinny fucking sparrow-like legs, you mark ma words ya wee rat.' Then turning back to the phone she'd continue, 'Ah, ha Sylvia, sorry you know what my lot are like, Jonny just needed tae ask something, now what were we saying Sylvia aboot the Bahaha hamas?'

We would all be laughing at Jonny, and even Lizzy eventually saw the funny side of his antics. For some reason she honestly didn't mind him taking her off now and then. When it came to my mother, Jonny got away with more than anyone else. I believe she always had a soft spot for his larking about. We all thought so.

It always felt like there was a release in tension when my Uncle Michael took over the phone call because Lizzy could really be herself again. Her shoulders would drop and her accent changed back instantly and the vernacular sounded normal to us: 'Fuck-sake, that's sounds great, that trip she wants tae take oor Gordon own. Iz he no a wee bit young fur awe this Mick, a mean he's only nine by the way, but if you think they really want him tae go, we know he'll be in good hauns.'

The next time I went south to England at Christmas break, the entire holiday was spent going over every detail of our Easter holiday adventure. Stephen and me would be locked in his bedroom, planning all the things we were going to do. Sylvia had got us guide books from the library and from her brother Danny, not to mention, pictures of his house with a pool. Everything else disappeared from the world. As far as we were concerned nothing else existed.

As I was returning to Glasgow I was on such a high I could have fuelled the flying Scotsman to take me all the way home at high speed without stopping.

That was the Christmas of 1971 and the New Year was being prepared for again with the usual gusto. Mother was in her kitchen, cooking, cleaning, moaning and swearing out orders to anyone who passed the open door: 'Don't drag dirt into my hoos if you go oot-side, ya filthy bastards ah mean it. Sammy, is there anything else we need fae the shops, they're gonny shut soon, remember it's a fucking holiday. Jesus, Mary and Joseph, could some bastard turn that fucking music doon, saints fucking preserve us; see these hoat fucking flushes am huvin, sacred, fucking heart . . .' Remember, she was still a Catholic after all.

It was a good Hogmanay and once again our house was the place for all the family to come and eat, drink and be extremely merry. The house was full to bursting with everyone letting go of the auld and ringing in the new. Grandad, or Old Barney as we kids called him now, was sitting in his chair in the living room, surveying the company: 'Look at all these stupid people, promising themselves they will change. I wish these fucking bells would hurry up and ring, so we can get this lot tae fuck off, sweet fucking Jesus help us.' There is something about the moment when a year ends and the new one begins. It's a special moment and Scots always want to celebrate it with great fervour and joy, with a show of abundance in their life.

Around this time I was becoming more aware of the curious sensations I was continuing to experience. Thoughts and feelings that often contained predictions. There was one particular occasion involving my sister Joan. It was like a vision. I remember I was playing behind the couch with some toy cars when mum and dad came into the room. They were talking about Joan. Her boyfriend at the time had borrowed a car and taken her out for a drive for the day. In the midst of their conversation I stood up from where I'd been playing and announced that Joan was in Carlisle at the police station and wouldn't be home until tomorrow. Carlisle is a long way from Glasgow, and since she'd only just left less than thirty minutes earlier, it must have seemed like a very odd statement. After a pause, they carried on their conversation. But that evening, when Joan was late home dad expressed concern and I was bustled off to bed.

The next day I got ready for school as usual and everything seemed normal. But it turned out that mum and dad had had a phone call from the police. The car Joan and her boyfriend had borrowed had broken down and they had been stranded somewhere in the Borders, so they'd contacted the police. As they couldn't get it fixed until the following day, they'd spent the night in the police station in Carlisle.

When I came home from school for lunch, Joan was back safe and sound. Nobody said anything about my premonition, and although I did feel odd for a minute, I just had my lunch and carried on as usual.

Precognition like this is not something you can use or control. It just sort of happens and each time it does, it can feel completely different. I had absolutely no way of knowing what was happening, or if everybody had such things happen to them. But to ask about paranormal happenings like seeing the future would just get me slapped. So I learned to shut up and try to work it out for myself.

It wasn't long into 1972 when I began to feel a deep-seated dread in the pit of my stomach every time our phone rang. I could not shift this sense of impending bad news. For a week or more, all was well.

It was a cold Sunday morning in February and our bedroom was freezing when we woke. We didn't have luxuries like central heating back then, so it was good to curl up and try to remain snug under the blankets for as long as you could. Besides, it was the one day of the week when my parents didn't get up at the crack of dawn. I hadn't slept well, tossing and turning and waking up in the pitch-dark room in the night. Now my mind was groggy as I tried to work out what had kept me from sleeping.

The phone began ringing loudly. I could hear the shuffling sound of my mother's carpet slippers moving quickly along the floor when for no reason, it felt like the bottom of my gut had dropped out of my body.

'Hello, Oh Mick, is everything ok?' From my bedroom I could hear Lizzy talking. My stomach started throbbing hard. It felt like someone was beating it repeatedly with a big stick. 'Oh, am so sorry Mick, aye, ah understand, I'll tell them aye. I'll call later, maybe aroon six o'clock and find oot wits happening, but I'm sure he'll be ok, try no tae worry too much, sorry again Michael.' The sound of the phone being replaced seemed somehow to amplify around my head. I knew something was very wrong with my cousin, but I dared not ask in case it was worse than I cared to imagine.

Stephen was in hospital having an operation on his stomach. The evening before he had slipped and fallen from one of the trees in his back garden. He hadn't fallen from very high up, but he'd landed stomach first onto a boulder and ruptured a muscle. He had some internal bleeding.

I remember that day so clearly. My family was quiet, listening to my father's calming voice as he spoke to us about it over our Sunday fried breakfast: 'He will just have a small operation. It doesn't sound too serious tae me.' Those words alone lifted a weight off my shoulders and a ton of gravel from my shattered gut. I trusted that what my father said would be true. My dad had always had answers up to this point in my life. He didn't appear to be too worried and what he'd said made us all feel better . . . but then I found I still had this terrible feeling in my stomach. The evening couldn't come quickly enough as I waited for the moment when my mother would call her brother and get some more information.

I know it might sound daft, but using the phone then was a kind of rarity and no matter what the subject was, calls were short and to the point and dealt with only necessary information. 'Don't be talking shite tae people own that phone Joan, remember it costs money, noo jest say wit yae huv tae and get oaf.' Lizzy would lecture anyone who wanted to make a call. Also, if you'd said you would call someone back at a certain time then that is exactly what you would do and not a second before or after the allotted time.

My mother had told her brother that she would call in the evening at six o'clock and that meant that no matter how worried she was throughout the day, she would refrain from lifting the phone until the said time. The family gathered in the living room with bated breath leaving the door wide open so that we could hear everything she said. No nonsense from Jonny either.

'Hello, aye, uh, huh, uh, huh, aye, uh, huh. Is that right? Well, that sounds better then.' Thank God! I had never known anyone in my life to have an operation and I was really scared until that moment when my mother said the words . . . 'that sounds better then'. Things were going to be ok and we would hear in a few days that Stephen would be discharged and all would be back to normal. How fantastic. Only that didn't happen.

When the results of the blood tests came back, there were

some abnormalities which turned out to be cancer. In the space of just several months, two people in my world had been told that they had it. My Uncle Barney must have been in his late forties and that seemed old to me and maybe even natural, but Stephen was only going on nine years old. How could this be? My head filled with many questions at the same time. How did he get it? Could it be fixed? Where was it in his body? Could it be removed with an operation? It was too much for me. As usual, when things like illness came up that were not considered suitable subjects for children, parents went quiet again. 'Don't any oh you lot go talking tae people outside oor family aboot this,' Lizzy said. 'Dae yae hear me?' We were told not to ask about things that didn't concern us.

But it did concern me. In fact it concerned me so much that I felt sick, really nauseous, as though I was feeling my cousin's sickness and somehow trying to take it away from him. Why couldn't I take some of it away from him? This was the first time I was conscious of wanting to heal someone. He was family, my best friend in the world. I felt a special connection with him and missed him when he wasn't there. He and I were going to the Bahamas at Easter, oh, what about the Bahamas? I knew much better than to ask anything about the trip when Stephen was ill. Such was the stress of that time that the trip was never spoken about again and just went away.

And Sylvia and Michael, what must they be feeling? Even though I worried for them, I knew I would never be allowed to speak to either of them on the phone during the Sunday calls and that the information that went to my parents would be vetted before we children got the version they deemed fit for us to hear. I was only nine years old, but I was experiencing a feeling of helplessness for the first time in my young life. I felt totally excluded and I really didn't know what to do about it, or who I could talk to.

***

Religion had not played a big part in my life up until then. I'd seen hatred between Catholics and Protestants in the street fights between football fans and rows between my mother's and father's sides of the family. But we didn't go to church. We'd watch posh families on the other side of the street dress up in their Sunday best to go to church and think it funny. I'd never thought about life in a religious way or about the great questions of life and death – or connected any of this with my own odd experiences of the supernatural.

Anna Barr was someone in our street. She was the girl who had told my mother about the Urquhart débâcle. Anna must have been around sixteen or seventeen when Stephen fell ill. She was a very buoyant, bubbly person always happy and cheerful. She talked to everyone she met, old or young. When she saw me sitting on the edge of the pavement looking down into a puddle she came over: 'Heah, wit yae daen Gordon, son? Is there something wrang wae yae?' she asked. I don't know why but I told her about Stephen and the cancer and his fall and that he was sick and that I was scared. And now I was more scared because I remembered that Lizzy had told all of us not to breathe a word of this to anyone outside the family.

Anna was one of those kind people who stand out in my childhood and I can still see her big, bright blue eyes looking down on me and hear her happy sounding voice as she pulled my arm up: 'Right come wae me, am gonny take yae somewhere and show yae something that might help, but don't tell anybody aboot this right?' Secrets, secrets and more damned secrets, my childhood was full of them, but I knew Anna meant well. I had no idea at first where she was taking me, but we headed off to the end of the street and round the corner to where the chapel was.

It was the Catholic church and Anna was a Proddy, a real die-hard, Orange Protestant. I thought she would never have entered a Catholic place of worship. It just wasn't done. But that is where she took me. 'Right, go in there and say a wee prayer fur yur cousin fae yur heart, tell the Big Yin what yae want and I'll nick a candle to light and that will make it work a think.' I wasn't sure what to do, but I found myself sitting on the back row of the pews of an empty church, looking around at all the magnificent statues. There were so many things to look at that it kind of blew my mind. My eyes were pulled in all directions, but came to rest on a statue of a woman. It was a big, grey, sandstone statue of a woman looking downward. I followed her eyes and saw that her feet were bare and exposed. I remember thinking she must be very cold. She *looked* cold. I gazed up at her face again and it seemed very sad, the way I was feeling inside.

I only knew the Lord's Prayer, which we said in school each morning, but I asked the woman I took to be Jesus's mother to help my cousin Stephen. I asked Mary if she could cure him and make him live and take away his cancer and help his mother and his father and could she make us still go to the Bahamas as well. I was lost in prayer and somehow I was starting to feel better inside. There was an overwhelming feeling of peace all around me. Something was happening in this peaceful sanctuary that I had never experienced before in my life. There was a pitch of stillness and I felt I was part of it for a moment. It was like being the actual sound that is in a bell when it rings out. I was part of something I couldn't see, as if I was being held still within something bigger, yet there was movement in the stillness and sound in the silence. It was perfect peace.

The peace, however, was shattered by a man's loud voice booming and echoing all over the place. 'Hoy, you, Anna Barr, get the hell out of here or I'll put the toe of my boot up your arse!' It was the priest.

'Run Gordon!' Anna had grabbed my arm from behind and tugged me towards the huge wooden front doors.

'Wits wrang Anna? Why's the priest shouting at you?' Anna stopped when she was just outside the grand wooden doors and out of range of our pursuer, then faced the angry priest who was still coming towards us. She was breathing heavily but smiling broadly as she put her two fingers up to the advancing man in black. 'Shove it up yur Fenian arse ya auld bastard,' Anna roared, pulling me away at high speed. But she continued to call out to the man who had stopped running just at the black metal gates outside the chapel, and he was shouting just as energetically:

'Get away ya Orange bitch, you're a heathen of a girl, God can see you, you know?' Anna was now laughing loudly and so was I. Her laughter was so infectious and I think it was great to feel the buzz of getting chased by the old priest. 'Fuck the pope and God bless queen and King Billy ya auld pape.' Her last insult fell on deaf ears as the man had turned and walked back into his house of worship. By now, we were too far away for him to hear her.

'Anna, if you hate Catholics why did you take me in there?' I was confused. The only time I went near the chapel was when there was a wedding on – as I say, all the kids in our area did, in the hope of getting money from the scramble as the wedding cars drove away.

'God's in awe the churches Gordon, he disny care wit wan you pray in its only they bias bastards who say who can come in or no.'

It felt like ages had passed and still there was no news about Stephen's condition. If I asked my parents or Betty, or Joan even, they would just tell me to wait, that the doctors were doing everything they could for him and we would hear better news soon. I started to have doubts about the prayers I said and wondered if God was Catholic after all as if maybe he didn't listen to Protestants.

Stephen's condition was getting worse and it was decided that he would be given chemotherapy. The cancer was located in the kidney now and though they did transplants back then, it was much rarer than today. Of course, I knew nothing about this. Neither did my brothers. All the older members of the family were keeping things from us.

It was still difficult for me to content myself with everyday things, but children have amazing abilities to keep going. For me that was following my two older brothers around asking them to play with me. 'Sammy, kin a play wae you?'

'Naw, fuck aff, beat it, go and play wae yur ain pals.'

Not one to give up easily I headed for Jonny. 'What ur yae daen Jonny, can ah play?' I would walk straight into the snake pit that was my brother's personal and very private card school.

'Goat any money planked anywhere?' he asked me, knowing I always had money hidden, usually under the corner of the carpet in my parents' bedroom. I would sneak in there when everyone was busy and put any coins I had in my secret hiding place. There were so many of us living in the flat that we none of us had private space so we all had hiding places. Jonny would plank his money and stuff it behind the cooker. It was a good hiding place, because no one would think of looking there – except my mother was meticulously clean and often pulled the cooker out from the wall to scrub behind it. Things like this would mean that you would have to move your stuff frequently, but for now, my plank was secure.

'Av goat a shilling Jonny, is that enough?'

Jonny would always strain his voice and hum and haw for a while before he allowed me to do what he already knew was inevitable: 'Ok, but don't tell ma we were playing fur money or ah wont let yae play again, dae yae hear me?'

'Aye, owe right Jonny.' The stake was a penny a game, but me playing cards with Jonny was like a mouse walking freely into a cat's open jaws. The game would be over in seconds, all my cash taken in one fell swoop. 'That's no fair, ah think you were cheating me!' More often than not, he was and if I found out for sure, we would end up fighting and screaming until mother arrived on the scene to pull us apart and demand to know what was happening. Jonny was a fast learner, though, and he soon realized that if he took all my cash in one go there would trouble and Lizzy would make him give me my money back. On the other hand, if he gave me little chances and extended the game over the course of the evening with me being successful several times, he could pretty much do what he wanted and get away with it too: 'Dae yae know, ah really thought you were gonny win that time, yae were so close, Gordon.' The sincerity in his voice made me feel good, believing I'd soon be able to beat my older brother at cards.

'Aye, next time a get money we'll play again if yae want.'

Sammy intrigued me. He was always sneaking different things into our house – usually things he'd stolen. I was fascinated by a collection of birds' eggs that he kept hidden under his bed in a shoebox, half filled with sawdust to pad the fragile shells. I used to love to take the eggs out and look at them when I was alone. Once again, there were endless fights among the three of us when it came to those eggs. This collection was Sammy's pride and joy and God knows, he had risked his life on many occasions, climbing tall trees and scaling buildings in the effort to collect them.

Sammy and I didn't have many fights as such, but Jonny and I did and he and Sammy would fight over almost anything, but when it came to the eggs, Sammy was very protective. Any little thing could set him off.

Once again, my brother Jonny saw an opportunity to make money when he learned how much some of the kids in the area were willing to pay for certain breeds of birds' eggs and also, how the fear of his eggs getting broken was a weakness in Sammy. All Jonny would have to do to make his older brother surrender anything, was to hold a little coloured egg between his thumb and finger and threaten to squeeze.

This would happen if Sammy had, for example, stolen boxes of sweets from a local shop. He would hide them under his bed, but if Jonny found out he would wait for the right moment to strike: 'Sammy, see those Mars Bars you've goat under your bed, ah want half of them or I'll tell ma da that you stole them.'

Sammy would be furious. He had my mother's temper. 'I've no goat any fucking Mars Bars, so fuck off.'

It was his natural reaction to lash out at Jonny in this situation, but just then, Jonny would bring out the kryptonite: 'See this wee blue egg wae the lovely broon marks on it, imagine how easy it would break if I jest snapped ma fingers just noo.'

He had learned that this wee egg was worth lots of money and was everything to Sammy. It was his prize possession, a guillemot's egg. 'Jonny, don't break it please, jest put it doon, I'll gee yae wit yae want, but gonny no break it.'

Jonny knew that his older brother was more afraid of the egg being destroyed than my father finding out he had stolen chocolate in the house. After a successful scam, Jonny would walk away feeling very puffed up, whistling to himself. It was a habit of his to chirp away when he succeeded in something I suppose. It wasn't long after the Mars Bar scam that he got a new nickname, Budgie. *Budgie* was a popular TV series in the early seventies, starring Adam Faith in the title role. He was always involved in some dodgy scheme.

We played and fought and scammed each other for money all through the summer holidays that year – 1972 was one of those very hot summers where the tar on the street would get so hot that it would melt. If you sat in one place too long your trousers would get stuck. When you got up you would notice your trouser seat would be very black and sticky – an offence that Lizzy deemed punishable by slapping.

Our street was filled from one end to the other with the buzz of children playing. Then a water hydrant would be let off by one of the older boys for fun and that would progress into massive water fights for all. It only took one splash of water over some unsuspecting boy or girl and mayhem would ensue. Everybody would run to get their mothers' empty washing up liquid bottles, fill them with water from the tap and run around soaking anyone they could find, until the street was ringing with screams and laughter.

When the ice-cream van entered the street playing its familiar tune, kids would fly off in all directions to get pennies or empty lemonade bottles which they could exchange at the van for ice lollies or cornets. This brought a lull to the bedlam, a moment of quiet as all enjoyed a cooling down period.

Music was often heard in the streets. Someone would put a radio, or tranny as we called it, out on the window ledge and turn it up for all to hear, tunes of the day like Dawn's 'Knock Three Times'.

How I loved those bright happy times. I believe that in the natural order of things, summer is a time of healing. It brings warm, balmy breezes to calm the soul and recreate our energies. Stephen was getting better it seemed and in mid-summer 1972 I got the best news I'd had in ages, when my mother came into the front garden to talk to me.

'Noo, don't get too excited, but you are gone tae London wae yur da.' As my mother continued, her words just became an extended buzz of the happy essence in the air around us and I couldn't hear her anymore.

'Yeeeeeeeeeeeesss, am gone tae London!' I shot out of the garden and ran up and down the street singing it out loudly. 'Am gone tae London, Am gone tae London . . .' I was so happy that I remember singing along with the song playing on the radio on someone's window cill: 'Last night ah heard my mama singing a song, oowee, chirpy chirpy cheap cheap.'

I travelled with my father on the train to London and we were picked up at the station by Uncle Michael who drove us home to Morden. We arrived late in the evening. Stephen and I immediately ran to the bedroom to play. All thoughts of his illness had gone from my mind. Since my parents had continued resolutely to say nothing about it, I don't think I even considered for a moment that my cousin was still sick. I didn't even notice the next day when my father left to go home.

Over the course of the next two weeks we played as normal with no thoughts of cancer. But, as the holidays in Scotland start and end before the English school holidays this meant I would have to return home in a matter of days. Stephen pleaded with his parents to let me stay longer, begging them to ask my parents to allow me time off school. There were a lot of phone calls between families over the next two days, but the upshot was that I *could* stay. Looking back, I think it was organized like that because my cousin was more ill than he looked.

The other news was that I was told I would be going to school in Morden when the term started back instead of returning home to Glasgow. I really couldn't believe my luck, how exciting it all was.

I don't think I ever saw my cousin happier than when we went to Box Hill. We slid down the grassy hillside on wooden boards we had painted. This was topped by a trip we had to the Isle of Wight. We travelled there on a ferryboat and saw a hovercraft in the distance. We stayed in a holiday camp for several days, playing games with all the other kids and we won prizes for races and even a singing competition. The entire episode was yet again the best thing I had ever experienced in my life. What never-ending joy. We stayed there till the night before the English school term started.

The following day I was put into my new school uniform and walked to school by Aunt Sylvia while Stephen stayed at home. She led me straight into my new class. It was not like being at school at all. The teacher was a nice young woman who was softly spoken. She just let us read, or she read to us. I lived with my aunt and uncle right through to Christmas and over New Year.

But Stephen wasn't the same any more. Rather than holding things back from me from me as my parents did, Aunt Sylvia sat me down and explained what was happening. She told me he was a very sick boy and that he was going to have to have a treatment called chemotherapy that might make him bad-tempered. While I was there that winter he lost all his hair because of the chemo. I demanded to be allowed to sit through it with him and remember being in St Helier's Hospital in Carshalton, talking to him all the way through his treatment, telling him about fights between Sammy and Jonny. Stephen loved to hear about my family and all the fights and crazy stuff that happened. As an only child whose parents gave him everything he wanted, he was fascinated to hear about how we earned money for things. I told him that I would go shopping for groceries for elderly neighbours and that they paid me three pennies for this. He couldn't believe that I could get money or lollies in return for empty lemonade bottles from the shops or ice-cream van. But mostly he loved to hear about the card schools, the buying and selling of birds' eggs and how they were obtained: 'What, Sammy climbed to the top of the roof just to get a pigeon's egg? Wow, no way.'

'Yeah, and he nearly drowned going out into the loch to get a swan's egg too.' (Notice my English getting a little better by now?)

'I wish I had your life Gordon, it sounds great and exciting all the time. My life is boring and I've got this stupid cancer.'

'My life is bad too, because sometimes I get really scared when people come to the door to fight with my mum, or Sammy and I had rheumatic fever and nearly died too.' I don't think we ever really noticed anyone else around us when we started talking like this. 'Heah, did a tell you aboot when Sammy stole the teacher's belt from his classroom?' When I came back home from school I would not leave his side for a moment, even when he was vomiting. My aunt tried to encourage me to leave the room when this happened, but I wanted to be with him and help him and he wanted me to stay with him. More than with anyone else we were connected.

There was nothing that would have made me leave Stephen's side back then, except for the pressure that my mother was putting on my uncle to send me home now Stephen was this sick. I did go home for a week, but Sylvia pleaded with my mother to let me return and stay for a bit longer. Her son was approaching his tenth birthday and he was dying. The only thing he wanted for the life he had left was to have me by his side. I was only ten myself, approaching eleven, but I wanted to be with him as long as he wanted me there.

No one, not even Aunt Sylvia, had ever spelled it out to me that Stephen was dying. It was not the done thing then to mention death, but everyone knew it, including me. But a child's eye view of things is very different from that of the adults around him and all I saw was my best friend and his smile when we played, or his laughter when I told him stories. Now when we played games like chess that he'd always been so good at, I would let him win, if only to hear his roar of victory. Yes, I knew that Stephen was dying. No one had to say the words. Somewhere in me I knew that I would lose his physical presence, but I also knew that what we had between us was a genuine force, a living energy and that could never die. I was more certain of it than anything else in the world at that point.

Stephen had his tenth birthday in April 1973. He and I celebrated it in his room with games of Subbuteo. I remember telling him how fantastic his birthday cake tasted, just before an impish look came over him and he found strength enough to push the remaining cake into my face, which made us both convulse with laughter. We laughed so loud and hard that Sylvia burst in the door with a look of terror on her face. She thought we were screaming with fear. That is one of the last memories I have of my cousin in this world. Shortly afterwards I was sent home.

His health went up and down for the next two months. One minute I was told that I was to go and spend a little more time with him and the next it was off. But by July there was no more mention of me travelling to England and people couldn't talk about Stephen without crying or at least almost crying. It was a hard time for all our family but for my sister Joan, who was getting married on 13 July, it must have been very hard. With all the stress of waiting for news from London I'm sure it was very difficult for her to go through with it, but she did and my Uncle Michael flew up for the day to attend the wedding. He was always very fond of Joan.

But this visit was the shortest I can remember. A phone call came telling my uncle that he would have to return at once as Stephen was near the end and asking for him. I went to the airport in a car with one of my sister's new in-laws. I remember the silence in that car. I was with two strangers and a man whose only son was about to die. The atmosphere around us was so thick and heavy it was like sitting in quick-drying-cement.

Stephen didn't die the following morning or the morning after that. His life force kept him in this world until the following week, Sunday morning to be exact. Again, I was lying in my bed as the phone rang loudly. It might as well have called out that Stephen had died, because no one ever phoned at that time on a Sunday morning unless it was bad news.

'Hello, Michael is that you? Michael I can't make oot wit yur saying can yae . . .' There was a pause in the conversation followed by a deafening silence. My heart stopped beating for a moment. 'Ok, Michael I'll tell them all and son, Lizzy will call yae later, we ur awe so sorry.' My father walked slowly back up the hall towards the bedroom where my mother was waiting for him. Her heart must have been in her throat. It was hard to make out as his voice faded to a whisper: 'Lizzy, that's it.'

7

Death, Dreams And Prophecies

All I could see were people dressed in black. No one seemed to notice I was there. I could hear muffled sounds, whispering voices echoing in what seemed like a vast empty church. And there were coffins. Three small, white coffins and several larger ones. Then there was a brown oak coffin and a bigger black one that stood out, and then I saw that some people were carrying another pine-coloured coffin on their shoulders. That was when the sound came from a far off distance, a horrible sound like moaning. It grew stronger and stronger, increasing in volume until it reached a pitch of reverberation around my heart. Aaahhh . . . I was sitting upright in bed, drenched from head to toe in sweat.

It was 1973 when Stephen died. He was only ten years old and I didn't know how to feel or who to blame. At first, I hated that woman I had prayed to in the chapel, and then I didn't because I remembered her son had died too. So I hated God instead. God hadn't helped my cousin or heard my prayers. He must be punishing me for something. And for a while I wanted to take the blame. Maybe if I felt pain of some kind, I might feel better?

'Gordon, your mother's on the phone!' My Aunt Sylvia was calling me from downstairs and I knew that it would be Lizzy telling me I had to come home again. I didn't want to go back to Glasgow. This was my home.

I had come to London with my parents for Stephen's funeral. I wasn't allowed to go to the service, but I'd stayed on after my parents went home. I wanted to be with Sylvia and Michael. They needed me to be there. I didn't want to go to stupid Glasgow where everybody just fought with each other, where you always had to hide things from your brothers otherwise they'd steal from you. And I didn't want to leave Stephen.

'I'll be back in a minute, Stephen,' I heard myself say, as I slumped my way downstairs and picked up the phone from the table. 'Hello?' I had to wait for a moment as it sounded like Lizzy was shouting at someone in the background. 'Fucking bastard, I'll be there in a minute and I'll punch the head oaf him. Hawd own a wee minute.' She came back to me and she was sharp. 'Right, noo you listen tae me, you are cumin hame at the weekend dae yae hear me? You've been there fur mer than a month noo and that's it. Av told yur auntie and she's ok noo, so don't be moaning at them tae stay longer, is that clear?' It was – very clear. 'Right, av goat tae go, some fucking teacher has hurt Sammy, so a better run alang tae that school and get a hawd ay the bastard. So eh, cheerio the noo.'

I remained mostly in the playroom for the last few days of my stay, playing with toys and finishing drawings Stephen and I had started. I could hear our conversations when I began to draw and sometimes I would find myself talking to him. It's difficult to describe, but the spirit of my cousin was still there, at least that's what it felt like. I might be building a Lego castle or a car and I'd ask Stephen what to build next. Years later Sylvia told me that she'd listen outside the door. She said, 'I used to feel happy. In your world Stephen was still alive. You were *keeping* him alive!'

Sometimes when I was on the floor drawing, or writing, his hand would rest on my shoulder and I could hear him sighing loudly. It didn't scare me and I didn't turn round. I didn't have to. Stephen was in that room with me and if I didn't look for him his presence got stronger.

People have asked me all my adult life if I was ever scared of spirits and I always tell them the same thing: 'Never, not even for a single moment.' Stephen's presence was warming and relaxing and the more I accepted him and allowed him to be close, the stronger our connection became.

Before I left on the Sunday morning, I heard Stephen speak to me. It was as if his voice was in my thinking and I was calm. It wasn't just me remembering how he spoke, because he told me something very specific. Clearly and distinctly he said, 'Gordon, help my mum.'

In retrospect, I can see that this was my first experience of hearing the voice of someone who had died. He asked me to promise his mother that I would be back sooner than Christmas time, when I was next scheduled to visit. I didn't know how this was going to come about, but I trusted my cousin.

For a second I thought about not saying anything to my aunt, but this made my stomach churn and I had a sense of something very strange happening. My inner self was also telling me I'd be back sooner. It was no longer the voice of my cousin, but a certainty that sat strangely in my gut. In retrospect, I can see, too, that this was another very important turning point. It marked my beginning to recognize and understand the inner or higher self which, if you are attentive to it, you will hear speak to you in an authoritative voice and which knows things that your everyday self doesn't know.

Now when my Aunt Sylvia looked at me, her brown eyes

were sad and empty. The life had all but gone from her face, leaving her without expression. To me she felt more dead than Stephen.

'We'll see you at Christmas then. And I'll call you every Sunday,' she said as she hugged me so close to her body that I could hear my own heartbeat.

I thought I wouldn't speak but words left my mouth without me knowing exactly what I was about to say. 'I'll see you in October,' I whispered loudly in her ear. Then I quickly pulled away and ran to my uncle's waiting car without turning my head to look back.

Before I knew it I was sitting on the train looking out of the window covered with raindrops at passing green fields. I was in a complete daydream until I said aloud, 'It's ok.' The elderly woman opposite me looked in my direction expecting me to say more. I looked back at her, but didn't speak. I was answering my cousin. He'd thanked me for telling his mother I'd be back sooner. The train rushed on through the elements towards Scotland.

Since Stephen's funeral five weeks before, I'd had recurring dreams about funerals and coffins and dead bodies. Death seemed to be everywhere since Stephen died. Charlie Bell, a friend who I'd played with on the garden path, was tragically killed when his family were on holiday. He was knocked down by a car. The whole street felt it. Collections were taken and people gave what little they could afford to help the family. As I've mentioned, this was something I remember happened a lot back then. Whenever somebody had a loss, my mother would go round all the neighbours taking donations and noting the sums in a little notepad. People didn't have much, but they always managed to share what they had in times of need.

When I returned to Balornock Primary I was told a boy in my class had drowned. Death appeared to come in waves and it was no respecter of age it would seem.

Alex White was the first of my friends to come and ask how I was feeling. He was genuinely sorry that Stephen died. His words meant a lot because he hadn't long lost his mother. But he soon changed the subject: 'Heah, did yae hear aboot yur maw, battering the teacher in the big school, it wiz pure brilliant so it wiz,' he said this with pure excitement. 'Teacher shat himself so ee did.' Alex continued to recount the story of my mother strangling a teacher by his tie while landing one on his chin in front of half of the secondary school pupils and teachers. Life goes on and all that.

Strange things were happening again. I would be playing like any eleven-year-old when my mind would freeze and some unrelated picture or scene would appear in my mind. Once I saw my sister Betty with another man. He wasn't her husband, but they were living together. The images were accompanied by some sense of knowing that it was true. It was a fact and that was that. A short time after this, Betty told my mother that she and Joe had split up and she was moving in with Jim, the new man in her life. As a child you don't tend to question things like this, especially when it happens in your head and you don't have anyone to share it with.

One Sunday morning in the beginning of October Jonny and I were playing a table football game that I had brought back from London. It had belonged to Stephen. Everyone in the house was still in bed. Then an overwhelming feeling came over me. I stood for a second in the hall where we were playing, just outside old Barney's bedroom. My breathing stopped for a moment and I thought that *something* actually passed through my body. I was speechless.

'Wit ur yae daen?' Jonny stared straight at my face and spoke in a forced whisper.

'Nothing, it's ok, just play on.'

He threw the ball back into the centre of the table and we both spun the handles connecting all our plastic players in an attempt to fire the ball at the opposite goal.

'YYeeessss.' Budgie's hands were up in the air and he was doing a little victory celebration in front of me. He had connected with the plastic ball so hard that, not only had he scored, but the ball had shot off the table and flown into our grandad's room.

'Budgie, you better go in and get that ball. You put it there,' I demanded, trying to force him to stop celebrating in front of me.

'Naw, the loser has tae get it, that's the rules.'

'Wit rules? You jest made that up the noo.'

'That's the rules, ma pal's goat wan eey these games and that's in the rule book. So unless you can tell me that you've seen the rule book, you canny argue wae me, kin yae?' I hadn't seen a rule book, but I was sure he hadn't either. Besides, I had never known of any of his pals to have this kind of game. But I wanted to play so badly and he knew it. 'Ok, I'm winning anyhow, so if yae don't get the baw oot ay Barney's room, av won the game.' As usual he left me no alternative. I could have just started a fight with him but we would have woken up the whole house and got battered into the bargain, so I went to fetch the ball.

The door was slightly ajar, but just as I went to go into the bedroom I felt a force field stopping me. I could see the ball. It was just in front of me. If I bent forward I could get it, but my body wouldn't move . . .

'Wit the fuck are you daen doon there, hurry up.'

I jerked forward suddenly and grabbed the ball, but I felt a sense of alarm. 'Jonny, something's wrang wae Barney,' I said to my brother quite spontaneously. 'I don't know wit, but he's not right. Yae better tell ma da.' Maybe it was the way I said it, but Jonny sort of peeked into the room. Facing my grandad's bed there was a dressing table with a big mirror that the old man liked to look into to see who was coming past his room. I don't know what Jonny saw, but he immediately alerted my dad to come and look.

Ma dad went in, then came out of the room slowly. Old Barney was dead: My mother seemed to sense it at once. Before my dad even got a chance to tell her she screamed out:

'Ma da's dead, I know it, I jest know it.'

'You two get round tae Betty's and wait there till ay come fur yae.' My dad spoke quietly but directly and we obeyed, shooting round the corner to Betty's flat. Jim let us in.

'Wits wrang son, is something wrang?' Betty was out of bed and wrapped in a dressing gown facing us.

'Barney's dead,' Jonny said, in a very matter of fact tone.

'Are you sure? Who told yae he was dead? Is ma da there?' Betty was now getting dressed, throwing on clothes from the night before. 'Jim you stay wae the boyz and I'll run roon and find oot wits happened.'

Sammy joined Jonny and me for a while and then eventually Joan came to collect us all and we headed back to our house. A wake was being prepared, to be held that same night. Blinds were pulled down on all our windows and mother was in full cleaning mode: 'There'll be people coming to the hoos soon, so you lot play quietly and tell yur pals tae stay away and huv some respect.'

'Ur wae allowed tae tell people oor randa's dead Mammy?' Jonny asked.

'Aye, ok, noo get oot and don't get dirty and remember, don't bring pals intae the path.' While Lizzy got the already spotless house even more spotless for family to arrive, my father took care of arrangements. He spent most of his time on the phone that morning.

'Wit did his dead body look like, did yeah see it?' Ian Harvey and John Barr were quizzing me.

'Iz yur ma sad?' Cathy Urquhart asked.

'Naw, she's cleaning the hoos caus lots ah family ur coming tae look at Barney's body.' Most of my friends were brought up Protestant and had never seen a wake, where a body is on view so that all the loved ones can come to pay their last respects.

'Dae they put pennies or the eyes? Ah heard they did that,' Willy Bell, Charlie's older brother asked.

In the evening our house was full to bursting with people, most of whom I had never seen before, and many I had never even heard of. There were the usual suspects, as well, like my Uncle John and his wife Cathy, who brought the Marshalls with them.

But of all of the people, two stood out a mile. Annie Barker and her daughter Frances. Annie was my grandmother Sarah's sister. She had married well, into an upper working class family and arrived by taxi. This was virtually unheard of in our street. She had a reputation for being classy and intelligent. But she was also tough. A force to be reckoned with. It was said: 'You don't ask Annie Barker questions. Annie Barker asks the questions.' Annie and her daughter came into our house walking side by side like they were actually connected. Both women were wearing sunglasses, beige trench coats and black, berry-type hats quite stylishly pulled to one side. They both looked like Faye Dunaway in *Bonnie and Clyde* and spoke with a sort of twang: 'Cousin Liz, sorry to hear about your loss,' Frances said to my mother, dismissing everyone else around her.

If Frances was aloof, her mother had an air of controlled violence about her that automatically commanded respect. She was a Glasgow legend and had a reputation for destroying people in seconds: 'Don't speak to me,' she said abruptly, holding her outstretched hand towards the face of Uncle John's wife when she tried to engage in small talk.

Undeterred, Alec Marshall tried to warm old Annie up. 'Mrs Barker, it is Mrs Barker? I remember seeing you when I was . . .' This time there were no words, just the hand to Alec's face. Then she broke her silence: 'Now, let me be clear. I came here to speak to my niece and pay my respects to Barney Davis, who was my brother-in-law. So understand this now, sonny, I don't do small talk.' Everybody got the message. Maw Barker had made her entrance, it would seem. Not even my mother questioned this Grand Dame of the Gorbals elite. I had never witnessed the noise in a room dissolve like that before.

As part of the wake, all the Catholic side of the family had gathered in the small bedroom where my grandad was laid out in his black coffin. My Auntie Cathy, after a few vodka oranges, decided to play lady priest. She gathered the entire Catholic contingent around the body and began to chant the rosary. I'm sure she meant well, but in our family, which was very mixed when it came to religion, all it took was one person to object . . .

'Listen tae these Fenian bastards praying!' People some-times think it must be nice to be able to foretell the future, but precognition is usually horrible. It shakes you up. I remember quite clearly being in the next room with my brothers. It must have been late, but there were still lots of people talking and then the voices all came from my grandad's bedroom and then it began. The buzzing, nauseating sound I had been hearing in my dreams was now emanating from the next room and my stomach began to churn. It wasn't like butterflies, more like a swarm of bees and I just knew something was about to happen.

What started as pushing and shoving quickly became punching and kicking. All the relatives left in the house got involved, either taking swipes at one another, or trying to pull people away from the fight. Uncle Barney, who was dying of cancer, had an ashtray smashed into the side of his head and was staggering about bleeding profusely.

My father told my brothers and me to stay in the room and not to come out. The brawl just got worse until I heard my Uncle John, who probably had the loudest voice among them, call out, 'Stoap it, ma da is falling out the coffin.' There was instant silence followed by the sound of something being moved.

'I swear I'm gonny fucking kill whoever started this.' It was Lizzy talking now. She hadn't been part of the brawl, unusu-ally. My mother had been talking to the Barkers in the street as they waited for a taxi to take them home. Like Lizzy, they didn't go in for all the religious stuff.

My mother was furious when she re-entered the house and began to punch and slap anyone who got in her way. 'How fucking dare you lot start trouble when there's a dead man in this hoos, am fucking mortified. Ma da's no even cold yet ya shower fuck-pigs. Gon, get oot ay ma hoos the

fucking lot ah yae!' I'll say this for my mother, she knew how
to clear a place.

Old Barney was buried a few days later, but of course
none of the young members of the family were allowed to
go. Perhaps the adults were worried that our sensitive little
souls would be upset.

But they hadn't bargained for my brothers, who could
never pass up an opportunity for a scam. During the time
that my grandad's body was lying in the coffin in our middle
room, Sammy, Jonny or both (neither wants to totally claim
this), snuck in and lifted the blind. They charged their friends
five pence for the chance of a peak at a dead body.

So glad my mother never knew that.

My Uncle Michael had driven up to Glasgow for my grandad's funeral and my Uncle Barney had travelled up with him,
but he found the drive too much for him and decided to return
to London by train. He was recovering from having his lung
removed because of the cancer and he was exhausted.

I was happy when I heard that my parents were going to
allow me to travel back with Michael in the car. I had a week's
school holiday in October and Michael had told my parents
that Sylvia was missing me very much. My uncle knew that
my visits lifted her spirits and persuaded my parents to let
me go for the week.

When we were on the road, it suddenly dawned on me
that what I said to my aunt before leaving London was actually happening. I had told her that I would see her in October,
not knowing how that would come about, and here I was
heading to London.

Over the next few years I travelled up and down to London
on every school holiday, but I never minded. It was like having

the best of both worlds. When I came to London I was treated so differently to the way I was in my own home. I was given anything I wanted – though I didn't ask for much – and I felt loved and needed. Especially by my aunt.

But it wasn't always easy. The price I paid for my London life was to find myself in the middle as my aunt and uncle argued. I had never known them to argue before. It felt as if each was blaming the other for Stephen's death. They fought about how much each of them was grieving, and that was hard to listen to. Sylvia would accuse Michael of not feeling the loss like her, because he had gone back to work so soon. Michael would make a big show by taking elaborate flower arrangements to the garden of remembrance where Stephen's ashes were buried, but then she accused him of not being able to talk to her about Stephen, that he was closed off to her.

In my own young way, I decided that their sadness was like the weather. There were days when it would come and hang over them both like clouds and I could almost see it around them. There were times when they wouldn't speak and the clouds thickened and it became harder to breathe in the house, as if all the oxygen in the atmosphere were being sucked out. Then naturally the thunder would come and they would have vicious spats about who loved Stephen more, or who was suffering the most. But, every now and again there would be a ray of light and they would be helpful and kind to each other or smile. That told me that the sun might still shine for them – and when it did, we all felt its goodness for a time.

After a while, going back home to Glasgow would feel quite good. This was a new thing for me because until that point I would have lived there for the rest of my life. But it was different without Stephen. As much as I felt a part of their lives, I had a natural pull to go back to my parents and brothers and sisters.

Oddly, I kind of missed the mayhem and the fights and arguments.

***

The phenomenon of seeing light around people was something I'd begun to experience from quite a young age. I could often tell whether people were happy or sad because of the amount of light that was around their heads and shoulders. I was certain this was normal. I always thought that everybody could see this until an advert came on television when I must have been about thirteen or fourteen. It was for a breakfast cereal called Ready Brek. In the advert they showed a little boy who lit up after he ate a bowl of this cereal on a cold morning, while all the other children had no light and looked very cold. I remember laughing and saying to Alex White, who was watching it with me, 'Oh that's funny he's the only one wae light roon um Alex, imagine yae had nae light roon yae?' My friend gave me a funny look for a moment because he wasn't sure what I was saying. It was only then, talking to Alex, that I realized not everybody could see this. I had no idea that this was some kind of psychic ability. In fact, I had only ever heard of such things once when we visited my mother's friend Ella in Blairgowrie in Scotland.

***

I was about eleven years old at the time. During our weekend stay, Ella's sister Sadie arrived. A sturdy woman in her sixties with short grey hair and brown eyes, she was a Spiritualist. After spending what seemed like ages closeted away with my parents, the four of them emerged from the living room with an air of excitement about them. I was desperate to know what had been going on in there. My guess now is that they had been holding a séance but I had never heard of anything like this then. That was when Sadie asked my mother if she could try some healing with me. I'd had an eye infection which wouldn't go away. Ella vouched for her sister and said that Sadie had healed many people and she sometimes got predictions for them too. I thought at the time that my parents probably went along with it out of politeness.

Anyhoo, it ended up going in a different direction. Sadie asked me to close my eyes and then she put her hands on my shoulders. Quite quickly after that I started to feel a vibration inside me. It was a good feeling, almost as if I was spinning. Then I started to see faces. Lots of different faces, but only one that seemed familiar. It was a woman who had big brown eyes and reminded me of my cousin Sandra. She didn't speak, she just smiled at me and again I felt good.

The vibration continued, then I became aware of Sadie calling out to Ella to come. 'Oh my God, this boy has clairvoyance, Ella, come and feel the power with him.' I remember wanting to open my eyes, but I couldn't. Meanwhile Ella's sister was sort of chanting, repeating the same word over and over again, the word was *clairvoyance*. I'll never forget how excited they both were. They said they could feel my aura and sense my energy.

The next thing I remember was this overwhelming urge to laugh at these two stout ladies dancing around me. I could feel Lizzy was present in the room with me and tried really hard to stop myself because I thought she'd get cross, but then it just bubbled out. When I finally stopped, Sadie asked me what I'd seen when my eyes were closed and I gave a description of Sarah, my grandmother. I now know that's who she was even though I'd never seen a photograph of her. I think mum just thought I'd made the whole thing up, but Sadie said, 'Have you any idea how gifted this child is?' The bottom line was she believed I was to be a great medium and that I would travel the world telling people about life after death and become a healer. Even though I thought it was rubbish, I did feel a wee bit puffed up that I was going to *be* something – even if I had already forgotten the word she'd used to describe it. But it didn't go to my head for long, because mother took me on one side saying, 'Listen you, get awe that daft shite that wuman said oot ay yur head right noo. Ah don't want you tae mention this dae yae hear me?' My brilliance was to be crushed before it even began.

Sometime later on that day, when things had settled down again, I overheard my mum and dad talking about what had happened while they were locked up in the living room together. It turned out that Sadie had spoken to the spirit of dad's dead father and had been able to describe him perfectly. She had also made a prediction. Dad wasn't working at the time because he had developed rheumatoid arthritis. But Sadie said he would go back to work later in the year. She'd practised healing on him, and although he would remain in some pain it improved enough for him to work again, which he did for another twenty years until he retired. All the predictions she gave dad came true.

8

Secrets And Surprises

Glasgow was a city going through changes in the 1970s. Many of the old Victorian tenement buildings were being demolished. This was great for teenage boys because old, empty, derelict buildings became great places to explore. People were being decanted to some of the newer housing schemes, leaving three storey vertical playgrounds for us to play in.

Of course, as a teenager, you know no fear and besides, there was also a chance to make money. Sammy and his friend Junior Wallace, a boy from our street, would often climb on to the extremely high roofs and strip any lead they could find. Many of us younger kids would be given hammers and other tools to pull lead piping from the old kitchens, as well as copper and brass. Sammy would bash all this metal with a hammer, because apparently it got heavier and so more valuable when you condensed it. Then he'd sell it to scrap dealers in the area, sometimes fetching a few pounds a time. This was serious money.

Days passed so fast back then. If I wasn't following Sammy around trying to earn money, I would be playing sport of some kind with Jonny and his mates. We all loved football, tennis and table tennis, but sometimes we would end up just having races. We would sprint from one lamppost to another, a sixty yard dash, or go longer distances. Four times round the block was about a mile. Most nights we would just drop into bed, exhausted.

Jonny was a great footballer, good enough to have gone professional, but life opened up a different path to him. He loved to organize sports. He wouldn't necessarily be the oldest kid in the street football team playing our rivals in Drumbottie Road, but he was usually the captain and often screamed and shouted at the rest of us when we weren't performing. 'Harvey, huv ah no telt yae tae mark yur man and stick wae um. Wan mer mistake and your oot the team.' A young Alex Ferguson in the making.

I loved sport of any kind. In school I was part of the swimming team too, and the sprinting and long distance running teams. As well as all that, I would play tennis with anyone who'd take me on at the ash courts in Springburn Park. Sometimes my brother Jonny would even rent me his football.

I had learned friendship from Stephen, and after he died my great friend was my neighbour, Alex White. He was a shy, quiet, passive boy. His mother had died of TB two years earlier and his father was very hard on him.

Alex was a kind and gentle soul and I found him good to talk to. We'd spend a lot of time listening to records – Bryan Ferry, David Bowie, Cockney Rebel – or re-enacting sketches from TV. Stanley Baxter was our favourite. At other times we liked to walk out into the countryside. Our walks could be ten to fifteen miles. Much of that might be over quite rough terrain at times, but all the while we walked we talked about things that teenagers were interested in. Sometimes we would talk about our families and how we both hated the fights and stuff that went on.

As my friendship with Alex grew deeper and the both of us more curious about grown-up things, we would talk more often about sex, the way teenage boys do. I remember that he had stolen a nudey magazine from his older brother and he showed it to me. I can honestly say it did nothing for me, and I really didn't know how I was supposed to react. I think I probably said 'Corrr!' a few times, and possibly even 'Check the tits on that, yeahhhh.' In reality I had no response to what I was looking at. I was perhaps more drawn to the poster of George Best that my sister had on her wall, but I didn't let that thought in.

No one really taught teenagers about sex in Glasgow in those days. In school there were diagrams in biology books, which the science teacher would tell you to study, but none of it was ever properly explained.

Sex education classes were taught by a very bashful science mistress. Reproductive organs or sexual terms were talked about in an embarrassed whisper, or she mimed the words like my mother. It makes me laugh when I recall how her voice was clear and strong until she had to use the offending words. Then she sucked them to the back of her throat on an in-breath: 'As you can see the man's pe-he–nis,' one hand covered her mouth while the other pointed to the floor for some unknown reason. 'When it becomes fully er-he--ch----t, before it . . .' The book was now raised in front of her blushing face. 'Carry on reading class, and no tittering . . . I mean smirking.' I always felt that if that woman had spent five minutes in the playground with us she might have learned some real sexual terminology.

Alex was a year and a bit older than me and he was much more mature than I was. He started to want to experiment sexually with me. I never really knew how to react or what to say in such moments, so I said and did nothing. Sometimes he would lie on top of me, fully clothed and rub himself against me. I never really understood what it did for him.

Alex told me that older men had abused him many times, though he never mentioned any by name. He told me that he'd been five when he had first been penetrated by one man and that others had performed sexual acts on him. Some of these men lived in or close to our street and he even said that one of his schoolteachers had touched him inappropriately at our primary school. Alex was a boy who probably needed attention, but I really don't think what he told me was some cry for help. It was shared in such a matter-of-fact way, like it was the norm for him.

In the late sixties and seventies there must have been so much of this kind of thing going on. You dared not say anything to anyone for fear that it would somehow be made to look like it was your fault, or that you had somehow instigated the act with an adult. As he had confided in me, I shared with Alex that I too had been sexually abused, telling him about the man who raped me when I was six.

So many people of my age, men and women are now opening up about sexual abuses they went through as children. I assume that there are many, many more who either don't wish to remember, or have just buried it so far down in the deep recesses of their minds that they genuinely can't recall it. As I write this now, the only abiding memory I have of my ordeal is the words this horrible man whispered in my ear when it was over, and just before I ran back to my front garden to join my brother and his friends: 'Now YOU remember this is a secret, it's oor secret and if yae tell yur ma, or da, ur anywan fur that matter, they will be angry at

YOU, and it wull cause trouble, so shussshhh noo.' He pressed his finger to his lips in front of my face and prompted me to copy him in making the shussshhhing sound. Even though I was only a child, I knew the secret this smarmy, horrible man forced into my young mind was very, very wrong.

I don't have any recall of the physical act that he performed on me, but my instinct told me never to approach that man again and I never did. Whenever he came to visit his relatives I would stay on our path. Something like a force field would build up around me, keeping me static. I remember asking Alex if the same man ever abused him and he said he did. I wonder how many other children he touched or abused on our street? He died when I was about fourteen or fifteen. A sense of relief flooded into me when I heard this news. His death took away from me the fear of being found out.

If my abuser was not around to tell people, then nobody need ever know.

***

Alex and I were having one of our talks one sunny day. We were sitting by the side of a stretch of water called Lumloch a few miles east of where we lived. We were watching water birds build their nests, so it would have been early springtime. The weather was good and all around us was the sound of nature, busily renewing itself. I was about twelve years old at the time. I don't know what our conversation was about but it was halted when the sound of loud barking could be heard coming from the wooded area directly behind where we sat.

We both jumped to our feet because it sounded like the dog was heading in our direction. We waited by the water's edge, both staring into the woods in front of us, terrified by the deep barking coming towards us. Then the most beautiful dog we had ever seen came out from among the trees. We now noticed the dog was wagging its tale with pure excitement. Neither of us had ever seen an Irish Setter before and we marvelled at the way her coat shone in the sunlight. She was a beauty.

We walked for hours around the small loch and through the woods, watching birds and animals, and all the time the beautiful Setter never left our side. She ran across us and then shot ahead and would sometimes appear out of nowhere just behind us, like she was working to some pattern. But we were now wondering where she had come from. A pedigree dog would surely be noticed as missing by its owner. Our best bet was that she came from one of the farms in the area and would head home when she'd had enough of us.

The sun was just starting to set in the early evening sky when Alex and I began to walk back towards the country lane that led to our bus stop and the last couple of miles of our journey. That was when we noticed that the dog was still following us. We tried to shoo her away, but she kept coming back. 'Ah think that dug is too far fae its owner noo,' Alex said, worried. 'Maybe we should take it wae us on the bus and take it to the police station in Springburn.' He sounded truly concerned. We both were, because we loved animals, especially dogs.

Alex had had a dog named Terry that we both played with, but she'd died recently. I was never allowed pets. My mother thought they were dirty and therefore wouldn't let us have one. I knew that when we got home the dog couldn't be taken into my house, so I let Alex take the responsibility for what would happen if we got it back to our street. That was the plan, but the dog – we were already calling her Lassie – had other ideas.

During our bus ride Lassie lay on my lap and went for a nap and as soon as we got off the bus she stayed close to me.

'Lassie, come wae me girl, cum own, this way,' Alex was struggling to get the dog to listen to him. Instead, almost as if she knew her way home, she trotted happily onto the path leading to my house and sat at the door as if she was waiting for me to let her in.

'Where'd yae get the dug? Did yae nick it?' Jonny was asking me.

'Naw, ah never stole it. It followed us hame and Alex is gonny ask his da if he will take it tae the police station and report it.'

Jonny wasn't having this; he knew how much I loved animals. 'Jeest be honest wae me and I'll help yae tae keep it, but it'll cost yae.' I should have known. Jonny didn't do anything for nothing.

'But Jonny, I canny keep it, ma ma won't ever let us get a dug. How would you change her mind?'

'Leave it tae me. How much money huv yae goat?'

The strange thing was, my father came home from work at that point and the dog shot off towards him. My father loved animals and animals, like children, loved him. Lassie was no different. I have heard many people say that animals know the people who are good to them. Well, in this case, Lassie had just found the one person who might find a way to get her through our front door.

'Hello there, you're a beauty aren't yae girl?' Lassie was running round him and then jumped up at him affectionately until he bent down to pet her. 'Oh you are the most beautiful girl, now what do they call you then?' He was smitten with her, just as we were, but I knew not to get attached to animals because Lizzy hated them with a vengeance.

'Da, we found her. Her name is Lassie and she followed us hame and we did try tae get her tae go back, but she woodny listen tae us and she came awe the wae here and Alex was goony ask his da . . .' The upshot of this story was that my father went to the police station to report the dog. But instead of taking her in, the policeman asked my father if he could look after her until the owner was found.

I was ecstatic when he came home with Lassie still by his side, and pleaded with my mother to let us keep her for the night. I have no idea why, but my mother looked at Lassie, who was so well-behaved that first day, and her heart melted in a way that no one expected. 'There's something aboot that dug and a canny quite put ma finger own it, but ok yae can let it stay fur wan night only.' I think my mother could never resist helping waifs and strays, no matter what kind. 'It will huvty sleep in your room Gordon, but make sure it disny go own tae ma clean bed covers, dae yae hear me?' I heard her loud and very clear, and was so astonished that I was to let this beautiful dog sleep in my room with me, that I was struck dumb.

The whole street had now heard about Lassie and everyone and his wife was now standing on our path listening to the story. It was such a buzz and my mother was quite right, there really was something about that dog. Come bedtime, I didn't need to call her, it was clear she was my dog. She followed me quietly into the bedroom, walked round in a circle a few times, slumped onto the floor beside my bed and gave a big sigh. She closed her eyes and I could tell she was relaxed. With all the excitement of the day and the miles I had walked, I was exhausted and was just about to fall into the deepest of sleeps when I felt a light pressure on the bed beside me. I half lifted my very heavy head to see what it was, but I needn't have. It was my dog lying in a heap beside me. I put my arm out of the bed covers and let it fall over her warm body. I had a new best friend.

No one ever contacted us about the dog, and it wasn't long before she was a real part of our family. She was a Smith in every way. Once she got in trouble for fighting with a neighbour's dog. Another time we had the police come to the house because Lassie had stolen a side of beef from the butcher's shop and on another occasion, she caught a mallard from the pond in Springburn Park and the Park Keeper sent the police to our house again. Lassie was catching up with Sammy when it came to being in trouble with the police.

Even Lizzy had accepted her. I think she liked the fact that Lassie could hold her own and in the end, it was just something else she could shout about. 'That fucking dug wiz on your bed again, av telt yae this, you ur no tae let it sleep wae yae. Wan mer time and its oot, ah meant it.' Lassie had come home.

I had never had this kind of closeness with any living being since my cousin died. At the end of a school day, she would be waiting outside the school gates and walk home with me. Having Lassie also meant that I didn't want to travel to London so much. I hated to leave her for long periods. I still visited during the school holidays, but it was becoming more and more uncomfortable as it was clear that my aunt and uncle were really not getting on. Then on one trip my aunt took me with her to a new apartment in Sutton. She told me that she couldn't live with Michael any more. The house was sold soon after, and before long my uncle had his own flat in Sutton. When I visited I would spend half the time with one then the rest with the other. I did this until I was fifteen.

Then thankfully they found a way to get back together and both moved into Sylvia's flat. For the first time in years I was aware that they had light around them again.

***

Some time after my fourteenth birthday, my parents told me we were moving house. I would be leaving Mansel Street, the place where I was brought up. I would have to go to a new school and make all new friends. It was the worst news ever, and I fought tooth and nail not to go. 'Ma, please just let me stay wae Betty or Joan until I finish school, *please*. Ah don't want tae go tae another school.' What was worse was that we were moving to the Gorbals and I really didn't want to go there, not after all I had heard about it as I was growing up. There were gangs and knife crime was rife.

It mattered not what I said or did. My father had signed the paperwork and everything was set to go before the end of the year. I was a passive child and rarely got angry, but now I hated the world and my parents and God and anyone else who happened to get in the firing line. I didn't want to be around anyone other than my dog and Alex White. Alex was fifteen and a half now and had just become a punk rocker. How he looked on the outside was how I felt on the inside. We were both going through a dark phase.

I hated my new home in Norfolk Court in the Gorbals more than I hated anything else in the world. It was a flat high in a tower block, dark with small windows. I had moved away from my friends, there was no garden to hang out in and on top of that, there was a danger that I wouldn't be allowed to keep the dog.

Everyone else in my family liked it. Jonny had left school that summer and found himself a job in a large baker's mill in the Gorbals and Sammy was working near there. Both my parents had jobs in the South Side as well, which is why they'd taken the decision to move, but I couldn't see that at all. There was certainly no way that I was going to the low-life, scummy school in the Gorbals with all the scruffs and down-and-outs.

I pleaded with my Aunt Sylvia to let me come and live with her after all, because she understood my pain and suffering. But though she offered to let me come down during any school holidays, she wouldn't encourage me to leave my parents. *So you won't do the one thing I want. So unfair!* I thought bitterly. I realised then that I was on my own and I became quite cynical towards her and my uncle, I recall. The entire world was plotting against me.

I dug my heels in and demanded to keep attending my own school in the north of Glasgow. But then I realized that I had to get up really early, go on two buses and walk for about a mile each school day, there and back. So I quickly packed in my protest and started school in the Gorbals after only one week's resistance.

I liked this new school immediately and immensely. I loved that it was a very mixed race school. The school I'd come from was all white but for one black girl. Here there were people from many different cultures, which was all quite exciting. I loved that there were not so many pupils, and that those who were in my class were really open and friendly from the very start. Even though I had gone with great reservations and the intention of being a loner, I felt like I belonged in no time at all.

On weekends I was allowed to stay with either my sister Betty or my friend Alex.

My friend was going through his own emotional turmoil at the time, which in part was about coming to terms with the fact that he was gay. I remember asking myself if *I* was gay, quickly shying away from what the answer might be. Nobody talked about being gay in Glasgow back then. You were a poof or a queer, and I pushed the thought down.

But when spiking his hair, wearing ripped clothes and severe black make-up still didn't make Alex feel right, he upped the ante one weekend.

One Friday evening I arrived at Alex's house with my dog in tow as usual. When I reached the top of his stairs leading into his hallway, he called out for me to stop where I was. I could hear his voice but I had no idea where it was coming from. The entrance hall was empty.

'Jeest stay where yae ur, am gonny dae it ah mean it so a dae, it's the end fur me and see how the world likes it.' I was totally at a loss as to what was going on. 'Alex, where ur yae and wit ur yae going own aboot?' His head popped into view out of the hatch on the hall ceiling.

'Don't stoap me ah meant it ah want tae kill myself!' I really had no time to think, let alone stop him, when like a huge stone he dropped from above only to make a loud thud on the carpeted floor.

'Aaaaahhhhhh!' He screamed in agony and I could tell that he had genuinely hurt himself. I shot to where he was to help him but it looked like he had done something terrible to his ankle. It was horribly twisted. In his haste to commit suicide in front of me, he had forgotten to double knot the washing rope which he had tied round one of the rafters in the loft and then round his neck. As he leapt out of the hole, his weight pulled the knot open and he smashed feet first onto the floor. He was crying with pain, but I couldn't help it and just burst out laughing. Then Lassie started to lick his face, which made him laugh too. It was all made even funnier when I noticed that his mascara had run and he looked like an anorexic punk panda. I almost wet myself. In the end I got ice from the fridge and wrapped it in a dishtowel and made an icepack for the stupid fool.

***

Flying through the air takes a certain amount of skill, I was to learn. One of my friends at that time was a boy called Robert Kelly, who shared my love for birds' eggs and things. He had a big German Shepherd that he walked for miles with me and Lassie in the countryside on weekends. One evening near his home, I watched a couple of his friends larking about on some scaffolding. They were swinging from one pole to another with great ease. I couldn't believe my eyes when one of these boys let go of the pole in an upside down position, did a back somersault and landed perfectly on the ground.

'Wahw, did yae see that?' I asked Robert.

'Owe, that's jest wee Stuart. He's a gymnast. He kin dae lots a things like that. Yae should ask him tae dae a backflip. It looks amazin'.' I was just getting my head round the word 'gymnast'. Wasn't that just for wee girls from Russia? And, what the hell was a backflip?

Robert introduced me to the two boys, Stuart MacMahon and Robert Davidson. It turned out they both attended the Springburn Sports Centre where they trained in Olympic gymnastics. They were both really nice guys and before long they were demonstrating their abilities on a patch of grass in the middle of Springburn. All around people stopped to watch them. I so wanted to be able to do the stuff they were doing on the scaffold poles. I was naturally athletic and so I watched Stuart and then copied him, building up a swing and then letting go of the pole at the right moment and rolling into a somersault. *This is easy* I said to myself.

Famous last words, because when I tried to copy their back flips something went horribly wrong. I remember flying backwards. I was in the air for longer than I imagined I'd be when I caught the ground in my hands and felt the weight of my body sink on my right arm. CRACK. I dislocated my elbow and slumped into a great heap on the grass.

My first attempt at Olympic gymnastics landed me in casualty where I had my arm very painfully pulled back into place, as my parents stood by my side. 'Wit the fuck were yae daen trying tae fucking fly anywae?' said Lizzy, unsympathetically. 'Is there something wrang wae yur head, boy?' Thankfully my father ushered her away from me. He could see the pain I was in.

I was kept in for the night and was let home with only a sling round my neck for support. It took me almost six weeks to be able to straighten my arm again. But I was a persistent kid, if nothing else. Most people would have run a mile from gymnastics or the thought of doing backflips, but not me. I wanted to learn how to do this properly, so I enrolled in the gymnastics class beside Stuart and Robert.

'Hey coach, this is the guy who did a back somersault from the scaffolding,' Robert was calling out to a bald man in a tracksuit, who was busy putting up a set of parallel bars.

'Not the one who dislocated his elbow doing backflips in the street?' I was now beginning to feel quite embarrassed.

'That's him.'

The coach approached me and asked to look at my arm. 'It looks like it healed nicely, so are you still keen to learn gymnastics then?' I was, and he remarked to another coach who had joined us. 'We've got a good one here, dislocated his elbow on his first attempt at backflips six weeks ago and he's back for more already.'

'I'll take him then, sounds like my kind of crazy gymnast!' The other coach, a man called Chris, was to be my mentor and this gym became a big part of my life for the next five years – not to mention, a place to burn up that deep-seated teenage angst that had been making me feel so dark inside.

I think of the next few years as very uncertain times. Things in our home were better in some ways than ever before. Everyone in the family was working and there was plenty of money coming in. I still had my dog, even though the council kept threatening to take her away – but for now she was safe. I really liked my school, was making new friends in the Gorbals, and I was training in gymnastics at least five times a week and sometimes more. All things considered, my life should have been good and it was, but there was something happening between my parents that made me very uncomfortable.

For as long as I could remember my parents had fought and argued with each other. But now they seemed to be *constantly* arguing, and that would inevitably lead to Lizzy throwing things at my dad and sometimes striking out at him. It was horrible to be at home with this going on more and more each day. I also became aware that my father was drinking every lunchtime. When we came home from school dad would be a wee bit squiffy. This would infuriate my mother. 'Huv you been fucking drinking?' Lizzy would rage.

'I had wan pint wae wan ay the boyz fae work Lizzy. It's no a crime.'

'Let me smell your breath.'

'Ahm no a child.'

She'd hit him. He'd never hit her back.

'Right well fuck the lot ay yae, make yur ain lunch am oaf.' She'd storm out of the flat and walk round for a bit. Or if she really exploded, she'd fight with my dad or anyone who stuck up for him.

In the evenings, I often took the brunt of these fights as my father would have had more to drink by then and mother would be livid. I spent much of my time trying to keep them apart. My dad seemed to find it amusing to antagonize her when he had a drink in him. I'm sure I built up some of the strength I needed for gymnastics by holding back the raging force that was my mother, when my father made some comment about how he had brought up her brothers and sisters.

I always felt so alone with this. No one else seemed to be around to help when it got bad. Both my sisters and my eldest brother had children and partners and were deep in their own problems. Sammy had got his girlfriend pregnant and she'd had a boy. But he'd chosen to take a walk on the wild side and struck up with a new girl, a very 'out there' American who just blew into his life. Her name was Grace. We called her 'Amazing', just Amazing.

As well as the increasing number of fights going on

between my mother and father, there were still the gang fights to contend with. Once a gang tried to get into our flat to attack Sammy. When Lizzy went to see off one of the young guys, he punched her so hard in the face that her glasses smashed into her cheekbone. Then a drunken mob burst in through the front door and started punching my mother. Lizzy wrenched the phone from off the wall and smashed it into the leader's head, where it shattered and became embedded in his skull. I had seen my brothers and some boys in my street use weapons on other kids, I'd seen people cut with knifes and blades, but nothing was worse than the terrible indignity of watching my parents try to destroy each other. They said things that penetrated deeper than any blade and left scars that would be difficult to heal. I think it was the most hurt I ever felt in my life up to that point.

'Your sisters are all sluts, whores!'

'Irish people are as thick as shit.'

'Your sisters are so short you could line them up under the bed like the seven fuckin' dwarves!'

There were many times when my mother packed her things to leave and one of us would plead with her not to go. We all tried to speak to my father in the hope that he might listen to us and curb his drinking. It all seemed so out of character for him, but you see, you don't know as a child what your parents go through and it can take years to begin to understand that. Sometimes you actually need to become a parent yourself to know some of the pressures involved both in bringing up children and in trying to be an adult yourself.

My parents had both carried their own sets of baggage for so many years. I don't think dad was in any way resentful about bringing up Lizzy's siblings, but sometimes he felt she had more time and affection for them than she did for him. Now all the unexpressed emotions collided and exploded, until one day it seemed that the fire was out. It was around the time when I left school, just weeks before my sixteenth birthday.

I remember coming home from a gymnastics competition one Sunday night. My parents were both sitting in the living room having a drink and laughing about the old days in the Gorbals. It felt like I had just walked into an altered universe or something. Lassie was sitting on my mother's lap and she was stroking the dog with great affection. 'Dae yae know something Gordon, this dug is the reincarnation of ma da.' *Ok, taxi for Lizzy,* I thought.

My mother was not a drinker. All through my childhood I could count on the fingers of one hand how many times I saw her take a small sherry, or a glass of stout, but it looked like she was getting well tucked into a good scotch with my father.

'Are you drunk Ma?' She looked affronted at my question.

'What, I've had wan wee drink wae yur Da and you think am drunk, don't be stupid boy, am jest saying that Lassie is moody like ma da wiz.' I couldn't ruin her happy moment. It wasn't often my mother relaxed and it was great to see. My father looked happy too. He was drinking but he didn't have that expression he had when he was trying to hide it.

Things definitely got better then. I was so happy to come home to a house that didn't look like a bad night in Belfast.

Sport was probably the thing most on my mind then. I was actually starting to do well, and my coach told me I that I would be entering the Scottish trials for the Commonwealth

Games in Auckland, New Zealand in four years time. I no longer had problems with my backflips. In fact since that awful episode I had learned how to do streams of backflips. I even learned how to put a somersault on the end.

And if you could already do a somersault, why not add a twist?

9

Teenager, Man And Boy

There are many potential endings to any life, sometimes directly and drastically affected by apparent small choices we make. I see that clearly in the case of my mum's cousin, whom I knew as Aunt Frances. (We met her earlier when she and her mother arrived at the wake both dressed like Faye Dunaway.) Frances went missing in 1976 when I was fifteen years old – it was all over the newspapers.

Frances is someone I will always remember and not just because of how she died. She was probably unhappy inside, but never let the world see her crying. She always had words of wisdom when you needed them and as a teenager growing up in our kind of family I was glad of the advice she offered.

In fact, she told me to get away. She had been there with her own family. Frances once told me that her elder sister Bridget was having a tough time with her husband. Because he had started to beat her, she was keeping away from the family, ashamed of her injuries. When their mother Annie got wind of this, she hired a taxi to take her from one side of Glasgow where she lived to the east end of the city where Bridget was – that would have been quite pricey back then. She then asked the driver to wait for her outside her daughter's house. She went in and without shouting or any signs of rage, beat her son-in-law with her fist until he slumped on the floor. Apparently, during the whole episode she never spoke until she got back in the taxi and said, 'Take me home now, driver'. That was Frances's mother all over, but sadly nothing in her mother's power could save her from her end.

Frances had been staying with us for a few days. She had fallen out with old Annie, which wasn't that unusual in itself and just needed to get away. I always liked it when Frances stayed with us. She loved to sing songs – one of her favourites being 'Killing Me Softly'. She would also show me how to dance and we would sit up late and chat. Frances was in her mid-thirties, but looked much younger. She was attractive and she was always stylishly dressed. She'd worked in the same job at a baker's since she left school and was known for never having missed a day in her life. She had the same work ethic as my father. As long as you can work, you never have to be poor.

Frances had her own flat in Glasgow. She lived by herself. The weekend she left our house was the last time we ever saw her alive. She went home to her flat before going to visit her sister Bridget. As the story goes, she and Bridget had an argument and Frances left her house in a hurry, grabbing her sister's coat by mistake in the heat of the moment. She hadn't noticed her mistake as the coats were similar. She jumped into a taxi in the street and headed home. It was late at night now. But it wasn't until she reached home that she must have realized that she had taken the wrong coat. Her keys were not in the pocket where they should have been. Not much is known about what happened to her after this. She was probably trying to get back to Bridget's, but we don't know. She was picked up by a man in a car advertising itself as a private taxi. The man's name was Thomas Ross Young and he killed her.

For the next couple of weeks her picture and the story of

her disappearance was on the front page of the papers in Scotland, and our entire family feared the worst. Frances liked a drink and she loved company, but never really associated with people outside the family. She had no man in her life – that we knew of – and didn't seem to have many friends. Her body was found several weeks later in a shallow grave outside Glasgow. This evil man was arrested shortly afterwards and found guilty at the High Court in Glasgow of killing Frances along with other charges of sexual offences against other women. Frances had been tortured, raped and murdered. He had stuffed clothes inside her vagina and set light to her.

The whole episode was like a heavy, dark cloud that just hung over everyone. It broke her parents' hearts when some of the things that their daughter must have suffered came to light. It was a tragedy that I will never forget and I often wonder how things might have been different if she had not gone to see her sister that night, or if they hadn't argued and Frances had stayed the night as she'd probably intended. Or even if she had just taken her own coat and ended up safe in her bed that night.

It is one of the very sad memories of my life. At the time, it was hard not to talk about it. Even though she was my mother's niece, all my friends at school treated me like it was my sister who had died. It was difficult to concentrate on schoolwork or exams, but somehow you had to. As a teenager you just keep moving forward because the future is waiting for you to get on the right path.

I remember thinking I wanted to go to college and study catering, or maybe work in hotel kitchens, learning to be a chef. My father would shake his head when I told him this.

He said that rather than wait for a college place I should take any job that came. He believed that I should get into the way of working as soon as possible.

But I didn't want to think this way. I had developed my own identity. I was different from most of my friends, even my siblings. This was partly because of all the time I'd spent in London. I'd driven around in my Uncle Michael's two-seater sports car, and my Aunt Sylvia had taught me to wear good clothes. I felt I was broadminded, debonair even and capable of doing something with my life.

When I was about fifteen Sylvia had taken me to see a film called *Little Darlings*. It was a teen film about sexual initiation. Lizzie would never talk about sex, so I was astonished when Sylvia asked me outright if I'd ever had it. Perhaps she could see how uncomfortable I felt because she went on to say, 'It's the people who don't talk about sex who get into trouble, and if a person is gay they should feel free to talk about it. It's not a bad thing. You don't need to lie.' If on some level I knew who she was talking about, I didn't admit it to myself. My life in those days was focused on gymnastics, not sex. In many ways, Sylvia understood me better than my parents.

But despite my fledgling ambition I was only out of school a week before I was travelling to a builders' merchant in the south side of Glasgow to work as a tea boy/general dogs-body/boy, go fetch things. I was paid a pittance – eleven pounds a week.

I told my friend, David from the gym, that this was a modern version of slavery. In my best arty fashion, I was sure I was better than this. We were into the New Romantics by then and cultivated the aloof, bohemian look. I liked the wit, the flamboyance of it, and David's wonderfully camp humour made me laugh.

David Highlands was one year younger than me, about six inches taller and he was one of the best young gymnasts in Scotland. He was dedicated to the sport just as I was, and trained every minute he could. David was like a light that lit up my life. We made each other laugh and really enjoyed each other's company. We used to love taking people off and doing little comedy sketches together. Just daft stuff.

David's family lived in Drumchapel, a housing scheme to the north west of Glasgow, similar in many ways to Easterhouse where I was born. But he liked to pretend he came from really well-to-do people and that he lived in a big house called Lillyburn Manor on the outskirts of the city. When he came to visit, my mother was completely taken in because he put on a convincing posh accent and he had all the airs and graces. 'Mrs Smith that salmon spread was divine, I simply cannot thank you enough.'

Lizzy would blush a bit and then she'd find that old phone voice. 'Auch, that's awful nice oh yae son, you'll be used tae eating the fresh stuff, ah imagine.' She would turn to my father and mouth, 'That's a lovely boy that is. What lovely manners.'

At my job I was smashing up old toilets and separating thousands of screws for a wage, but all of that just disappeared when I could get into my sports gear and warm up for the rings, or parallel bars, or high bar, or vault. My favourite discipline – as was David's – was the floor exercise. We'd be tumbling, doing flips and somersaults, adding twists to make the move more skilful, while keeping it controlled and graceful.

It gave me a sense of pure and uncontaminated joy to express myself through these daring and athletic movements. For me, gymnastics was a mental discipline as well as a physical work out. The focus you needed in order to swing around the high bar, let go, twist in mid-air at high speed and re-catch the bar again demanded precise concentration. Now, when I give talks on meditation, or any spiritual practice, I tend to think back to those days when the physical and mental faculties had to synchronize perfectly, and I wonder if that skill was a planned part of my life's journey.

Out of the gym and away from David, I was like a fish out of water. I remember feeling that I didn't fit in with many people. When I was sixteen, seventeen I always felt awkward unless I was spinning round a pommel horse, or in a tracksuit stretching the muscles in my body till they burned.

Meanwhile friends like Alex White had abandoned punk and were getting into disco. Music then was even better if you bought it on coloured vinyl, and twelve-inch singles were an absolute blast. *Saturday Night Fever* had blown everybody away. It was around this time at a party at Alex's house he told a group of us that he was gay – and that he fancied John Travolta.

It was great news that Alex was gay, because it meant that he would stop making feeble attempts to kill himself. During one of his earlier disco parties, BG (Before Gay), Alex had shut himself in his bathroom and demanded to be alone. We all took him at his word and ignored him. Then he began to pound the frosted glass on the bathroom door and shout loudly that he had cut his wrists with a broken glass. I eventually got in beside him and saw that his arms were running bright red. I was scared for a moment and then I noticed the familiar smell. 'Alex, is that tomato sauce own yur arms?' It was. He had taken the bottle in with him and dowsed it all over his wrists and arms.

Everybody my age was drinking back then. I was too into my sport. I also thought that alcohol meant fights, as it certainly did in my family. The world and his wife smoked fags in those days and I remember, too, that I hated cigarette smoke in my teens. I even told my mother off for smoking, lifting up a filthy ashtray and telling her, 'This is what your lungs are like, Ma.' My mother hated to be told this, because she knew it was the only thing in the house that was dirty.

Despite feeling a bit of an outsider, I stuck with my routine. I worked at the builder's yard, went to the sports centre almost every evening and walked my dog. I liked Alex, but I didn't think I was gay. I liked David and his camp humour, but I wasn't sure if he was gay. I kissed girls in my teens and told all my friends that I had had sex when I was fifteen, the thing to do. I could just make up any girl in London and tell a sexy story about her. I was still going back there almost every holiday.

Then along came Katie McIver and a whole load of cheek. When we met we argued. We didn't like each other and found any reason to slag each other off. She'd say of my dog, 'Is this your girlfriend?' I'd say, 'Well, she's better looking than you.' Katie was blonde and beautiful with brown eyes from her Italian blood. She had the best legs I'd ever seen, and she was very popular.

We would argue and then laugh. Her humour was very dry. She was a great mimic. She could listen to anyone and take off their character in an instant. She was different to other girls.

She even stood up to my mother. When they first met there was a flare up and Katie said, 'Come on old woman, have a go if you think you're hard enough.' I was speechless with anxiety – and admiration.

If I remember correctly, she was going out with Ian Harvey. I say going out but all it actually involved was kissing for hours. Yes, *actually* hours until your mouth was anaesthetized and limp. In Glasgow they called it winching.

Katie and some of her friends used to walk me to the bus stop late at night when I caught the last bus back to the Gorbals. I'd have Lassie by my side. I remember thinking how much Katie irritated me, so I have no idea how we came to be kissing on the stairs at the bottom of Alex White's hall one night. I think we sort of dared each other. But after that, we were going out, I suppose. Every night after that we spent hours locked in winching. It was perhaps a relief to some of my family that I had a girlfriend as I am sure they must have suspected I was gay. After all, my friend Alex had come out.

I always hated telling my family anything I was doing back then. It was like it was my business and I got awkward and very testy if people asked me personal questions. 'Gordon, ur yae winching anybody the noo, son?' an uncle or aunt would ask. I would blush and try to exit the room without answering.

I was seventeen when I first started going out with Katie, a year older than she was. Now that we were an item it was even harder to find time to fit everything into my very busy life.

★★★

The city council had written to my parents about our keeping a dog in the flat. Lassie was part of the family and even Lizzy would have fought for her, but eventually two officers came round. They told my parents to get rid of the dog or they would be served with an Eviction Notice. They had no alternative but to let the dog go. So she went to Tommy's. I told myself that this would be better for her because my brother had a house with a front and back garden. Lassie would live out her last days with him and his children and have much more freedom.

I say this, but my heart was broken. I didn't want to lose her. She was really my best friend in the world. Even though I put on a brave face it really affected me badly. I would phone my brother every day at first to find out how she was. I was always told the same thing: 'Gordon, the dog is happy, awe the waens in the street love her and play wae her every day and she loves running over the fields wae us.' It helped to hear this I must say, but I was soon to have other things on my mind that would have to take precedence.

'Gordon, ah think am pregnant?' When Katie spoke these words they hit me like one of Lizzy's fists. I could find no words. All I could think of was, *How?* I wasn't so naïve as not to know how she had gotten pregnant. In fact I remember enjoying the process, but I think my question to myself was more: 'How could you let this happen?' I was only eighteen. Of course we never used any birth control, me because I didn't know I had to and Katie because she was Catholic and didn't want to go on the Pill. But worse than that, we never even spoke about it. We were Glaswegians in 1980, 'yae didny talk aboot fings like rat, ren.' Now that's good Glaswegian.

That stupid biology teacher, I thought, why hadn't she taught us better? Like many young people Katie and I found we were parents-to-be when we weren't really adults ourselves. We hadn't even been going out together for a year. We hadn't done things that courting couples do, like go on holidays together or have romantic dates and live out all the giddy, being-in-love kind of experiences. We were definitely 'in love' because we did all that crap of phoning each other every minute of the day – and this was before mobile phones. I used the work phone whenever no one was around to ask Katie how she was feeling five minutes after I had just asked her. Then we went through all that, You hang up, No, you hang up. But now it had all got very serious, not to say scary. We were trying to decide what to do next, without telling her parents and, oh my God, Lizzy! In the end, Katie's mother Josephine and her stepfather Bob, were actually ok and quite supportive – after the initial telling-off about responsibility and all that. They were Catholic after all, so maybe thought they might as well blame the Proddy. I didn't mind, I would have flogged myself with worry beads if it had made everything seem normal again.

Telling my parents was horrible for me. The sense of dread was quite sickening. I don't know why because both sides of my family were no saints. There were children born out of wedlock left, right and centre, not to mention divorces and separations to boot. Somehow, though, that walk of shame alone down the hall to the living room in my parents' flat in the Gorbals, seemed unbearably longer and the presence of my parents sitting there felt huge. Even worse, though, was their reaction to the news that their youngest was going to be a father. There was none. As soon as I walked in Lizzy said, 'You don't need to tell me. I know exactly what you are going to say,' and then she just stared right through me. I would have given anything for one of her outbursts of rage. Even if she'd lashed out at me it would have been better than that silence. My dad didn't speak either. He just sighed like he was expecting the news and shook his head and shrugged his shoulders.

But it was over. I left their house at high speed to go to Katie who was waiting for me round the corner. I think it was then that I realized that I might have been going out with the mirror image of my own mother when she told me what she thought. 'Oh well, if she's no interested, then she can go fuck herself!' OMG.

Katie and I decided to make the best of it. We really loved each other. We were like brother and sister.

When I first met Katie I had lots of money for someone in my position. Everyone in our house was bringing in money so Lizzy let us keep most, if not all, of our wages. I was getting twenty-two pounds a week in the builders' merchant and had a drawer in my bedroom with several months wages unopened. Plus I always had money from my aunt and uncle in London. My bank account was quite set, I recall. Not for much longer though.

A pregnant girlfriend has many needs, I found out. 'Eh, ah think we need tae get this pram, it's the new wan and this cot . . .' The list went on and on. There were outfits chosen to go into hospital and others for coming out, and there were many choices of outfits for the baby as well. It wasn't long before my drawer was opened and the wage packs started to go down. I lost my job in the builder's merchant due to lay-offs just weeks before my son was born, and that meant that we had to get by on the savings I had, which were, of course, fast running out. I would have to find a job pretty quickly.

The great sadness for me in all of this was having to give up my hopes of becoming a star gymnast. It's often said that the only escape routes out of a place like the Gorbals are through sport and show business. A letter came telling me that I'd been chosen to be in the squad for the

Commonwealth Games. That didn't mean that I was definitely going, but that I had a very good chance. I'd had a dream that I'd shared with my friends at the gym, and now I was ashamed to have to tell them I was giving up on it, because I'd got a girl pregnant. (David would find his escape route. He went on to dance for the Ballet Rambert but later, I heard, he died of AIDS.) In my intense disappointment I was perhaps experiencing something of what Lizzy had gone through when her mother died. She'd had to give up her dreams of show business to look after family.

My Aunt Sylvia and Uncle Michael went kind of quiet on me at this time. I found out later that they were disappointed in me because they'd hoped I would come to London where they had a life all mapped out for me. The plan had been that I would work with my uncle in his roofing business and they would buy me my own flat and car and all of their possessions would be mine someday. Sylvia didn't speak to me much when I called her after this, and for some reason it felt like I had been drummed out of the Brownies.

But it was the path I had chosen. Sticking with Katie and going through with the pregnancy was the best decision I ever made. It was a scary one, but no one said life was easy.

Five minutes ago I'd been about to compete for my country as a gymnast, now I felt like a little boy among men. Katie had gone into labour and I was sitting in the father's waiting room in Stobhill Hospital nervously hoping for news. It was 14 June 1981 and there was a guy sitting opposite me called Jonny Murphy. I knew him from Drumbottie Road, the road that ran parallel to Mansel Street. His wife was in labour at the same time and I watched him as he chain-smoked. I particularly remember the hypnotic way he turned the fag around and around in his fingers between puffs. 'Dae yae want wan, Gordon?' Jonny kindly offered me one of his John Player Specials. I didn't smoke, but I took one, more as an automatic reaction than out of need. I had tried smoking by this time and hated it, but at this moment it felt right.

The fourteenth of June became the fifteenth and Jonny was called away from the waiting room. His wife gave birth to a daughter in the early hours. I remember how ecstatic he was when he ran back in. He told me it was the most wonderful thing he had ever witnessed. He was crying and I hugged him.

'Yuv goat tae go in and see it, man. Am no kidding, it's amazing. Ur yae gonny go in and be at the birth?' Honestly Jonny, I wasn't even sure I should have been at the conception, man.

'Naw, am gonny wait in here,' I said to him. I was excited for him and I was very scared for Katie. All of a sudden it dawned on me that she might be frightened and she was on her own. But she didn't want me to be beside her. She was very funny about that, after all she was just approaching eighteen.

Jonny left the hospital and I was the last person in the room. A nurse passed up and down and every time I looked at her for news she shook her head with a sympathetic look on her face. It stands out in my memory that she was singing quietly to herself, a Michael Jackson song that was a hit then, 'One Day in your Life'. I always associate that song with my son's birth, which happened close to four o'clock on the morning of the 15 June 1981. 'It's a boy,' the nurse said with a smile on her face as she showed me into the delivery room where Katie was lying, looking very exhausted. But she smiled as she showed me our son and something moved in me that was like being touched by God. A vibration in and around my body made me feel huge and limitless. I cannot explain what it felt like when I saw and felt the presence of Paul for the first time.

'That was that,' Katie said to me when it came to his name. She was always going to call our baby Paul if it were a boy. I would have been able to choose a girl's name which would have been Nicola or Sarah, after my mother's mother, whom I never met. But Paul it was. You can see that the whole psychic thing hadn't truly kicked in yet.

For the first few months of Paul's life, Katie and I lived with her parents. Katie's grandfather, Joe Gargano, was a barber and he told me that some relative of his was an instructor at one of the hairdressing colleges. They were paying thirty-five pounds a week to people who went on the new government training courses. That was more than I had been getting at the builders' merchant and it sounded easy enough. I had never even thought about hairdressing, but now I could get paid and trained in something at the same time and it was nine-to-five Monday to Friday. Katie and I had just been offered a newly renovated flat in Drumbottie Road, so taking the course would mean we would be able to afford it and we would have our own home – me, Katie and Paul.

Old Joe took to our son the moment he first laid eyes on him. I won't ever forget how he helped us with money and how willing he was to look after Paul when Katie got little jobs here and there, in shops and such.

It is frightening being a new parent and a very young new parent at that. I remember that I would sometimes stay awake all night long just looking at the baby. I was afraid he would stop breathing or something. I would get paranoid anytime his breathing went soft or quiet. I would poke him with my finger gently, just enough to stir him till I was satisfied he wasn't dead. Every parent has these concerns, but no matter what people tell you, you will worry for your new-born and then on and on and it really never ends.

When I first started my new course in Queenslie Skill Centre, where I went to train in gent's hairdressing, I remember thinking it would all be a bit of a laugh. But by the second week I was really fascinated. My instructor was a man named Davy Wahl, who was a very good, all round hairdresser. He saw potential in me and decided to teach me much more than the simple course entailed. He brought in dummy heads and taught me how to do ladies styles and perms, which were all the rage in the early eighties. He also gave me much more than the basics in clipper cutting, which was about all most people learned from the course.

But then death crossed my path once more. On Mondays we had old age pensioners come to the training salon for their free haircut. Normally, one of the newbies would start and then let one of the more advanced students finish it off, or even Mr Wahl, if need be. This particular morning I had an old gentleman sit in my chair and I offered him the usual consultation. 'How much dae yae want aff yur hair then, Mr?' It was a class joint, as you will gather.

'Short back and sides son, square neck if you don't mind.' I didn't. It was easier to make a line at the bottom of someone's neck with the clippers than fade the hair out to a tapered look. I clicked my long barber's blades several times and I was off, snipping furiously, the soft grey hair flying into the air like fluff from a dandelion.

'Are yae jest oot for a haircut, or are yae going somewhere nice sir?' Nothing. I thought he was probably hard of hearing. 'Can yae jest lift yur head fur me a wee minute sir and tae ah square the hairline sir?' Still nothing, so I did the best I could as his head drooped onto his chest. I got my thumb and forefinger and gently raised the man's brow. 'Sir, kin yae jest keep yur head up fur a wee minute please?' Davy Wahl knew by this point that something wasn't right and rushed over to my cutting station. He studied the situation for a minute and realized that the man was already dead, or in a very deep coma. He called for an ambulance, and when it arrived they just confirmed his diagnosis. My first full haircut and I killed my client. It was all over the college. They were calling me Sweeney Todd. I had never finished a full client on my own till that point, now I had just finished one off.

My time in the hairdressing class was filled with laughter. I learned that hairdressing is a great setting for comedy and it started me off on one of the best parts of my life. From that little government course I would go on to work in all aspects of hairdressing for the next twenty-three years, loving every moment of it. After only nine months I got my certificate and was sent out into the salons of Glasgow to work my magic.

Talking of magic, it had been years since I had any experiences with other worldly things. I believe that during your teenage years access to this inner world is closed down. I mean, I hadn't had any funny dreams or premonitions for ages and I hadn't even thought about that stuff if I'm honest. But when I first moved into our new flat on my own to get the place ready, I ran into someone I hadn't seen in years.

Katie and her mum had been in our flat decorating and getting it ready for when we could afford furniture and she would be able to move in with the baby. At that point all we had in our new flat was a cooker, kettle and a very small fridge. In the bedroom was a double bed and a chair on which sat a digital radio alarm clock.

The entrance to our tenement building had a security door on it, but everyone in Drumbottie Road knew me and Katie. Though it was a rough street, people had nothing worth nicking, so I was contented to sleep there alone for now.

One night I went to bed and just after I had set the alarm for the next morning I thought I heard someone on the stairs leading up to the landing above me. This was strange because the flat above was unoccupied and boarded up. I listened for a moment and then must have drifted off into a sound sleep.

It was four o'clock in the morning when I woke. My clock was flashing the time the same way it would have if the alarm had gone off. But the alarm had been set for seven o'clock, so this was bizarre in itself. My senses seemed to expand and fill the room. It was as if I could feel every atom in the atmosphere – and as if someone was standing beside me. I knew without looking. There was a woman there. My pulse was racing, yet I wasn't scared in the least. It felt natural, but exhilarating. I could hear someone breathing very hard and then noticed it was me, the person that was lying in bed. I was in an out of body state looking at myself and at a woman standing, looking down at me as if watching over me, caring for me. She looked about the same age as me, in her twenties, but it wasn't like she was there in the flesh as Ummy had been. She was a light-being, luminescent like a hologram only brighter and radiating a sense of well-being. I knew she was Ummy's girlfriend, my mother's mother, Sarah Riley. I felt safe with her, in fact there was never any sense of fear at all.

The moment I realized that I was in two places at once I was shot back into my body and there was an almighty noise in my ear. It was like chalk breaking on a blackboard and it scraped through my very being until I jumped up in bed. I felt like I had been injected with adrenalin. My entire body was vibrating. Something told me to put my feet on the floor and ground myself.

This was one of the strangest things that had ever happened to me and I had no way of explaining it. I knew that I didn't want to tell Katie about this experience as it might frighten her and put her off moving in to our new place. So who exactly could I tell? The people at work? It would sound mad, whoever I told, so I chose to tell no one.

When people have big emotional events in their lives, spirits are released. Well at least I believe now that's what happened to me.

10

Hairdressing, Husband And Holiday From Hell

The early part of our marriage was pretty much like anyone's. We were still very much in love and probably too attached to one another to notice the world outside us, but it wasn't long before that same world forced its way into our lives. Drumbottie Road had been a part of my life when I was growing up. It felt very familiar and once we started to get enough money to furnish our flat properly we really began to feel at home.

The street was full of people in much the same boat as us. There wasn't much of anything to go around. Somehow or other Katie, Paul and I could managed to eat on a pound a night. Most people in that street were struggling, but everyone would have given their last penny to help someone else out, because it wouldn't be long before they would be the ones asking. That's just how it was.

Our new flat had a bay window that allowed us a good all round view of the street. We saw some of the many dodgy goings on that took place in corners in the tenement closes and sometimes in the middle of the street in full view. Initially it was the exchanging of shoplifted and other stolen goods; there wasn't a big drug problem when we first moved in. Those who would eventually descend to addiction were experimenting with glue and cheap booze at this time.

But not one person in that street would have harmed a

hair on any of our heads and though conditions might sound bad, things seem very different when you are on the inside looking out.

Windows were important on that street. Most communication was done through the open windows: 'Hey Katie, huv yae goat any sugar ma ma can borrow?' Or, in many cases, 'Katie, can yae lend ma ma a couple ah pounds tae she gets hur Giro?' A common call from the windows of Drumbottie. It wasn't only words that were exchanged through windows; goods would be passed from one neighbour to another and sometimes those in the third floor flats would drop objects to be caught by someone down below, rather than climb down all the stairs. The constant use of our windows meant that when children were playing in the street, an adult could always see them. Nothing went unnoticed in that world.

Each day Katie's mum, Josie, would come and collect Paul and take him out for the day to her father's house, where old Joe treated my son like a little prince. Joe's house was always full of people coming and going and they all loved to spoil Paul, who was a very contented child.

I was working in a little salon in the east end of Glasgow, getting paid five pounds a day plus tips. At the end of the week, I'd earned just slightly more than I got for attending college, and that was only if the tips were good. I was employed to do gent's styling, but I found that I was getting better at women's hairdressing, which Linda, my new boss, encouraged me to do. Ladies hairdressing came easily to me and I soon learned that I could do 'homers', where I went round to people's houses in our street. I did haircuts for a pound and perms, highlights and tints for a fiver, much less than they would pay in a salon. The extra money I was making from this meant that we had a slightly better standard of living and things actually seemed to be going well. The disadvantage was that my home hairdressing was becoming so popular that sometimes I didn't get home until very late at night, and soon it began to feel as if my whole life was taken up with work. I didn't have a car then, so I would find myself walking round with three big bags full of hairdressing equipment, one of which held the overhead dryer I needed for the perms and highlights. It was a tough old slog I suppose, but I didn't really feel it at the time because I loved hairdressing. I had a passion for it and a flair. It sort of brought out my artistic talents.

One day, a pensioners' day, an elderly woman came in for a perm. Linda was busy with several clients. Moving from one to the other she asked me if I would cut this lady's hair ready for perming. This wasn't a problem. It was a simple layered haircut – what could go wrong?

The old woman's hair was very knotted when it was wet. You couldn't put conditioner on the hair before perming, so it was common that you'd have to spend some time combing the hair through until all the knots were free. I then layered the hair so that it was the same length all over, ready for perming. All I had to do now was find out how long the lady wanted the hair at the back and sides. I asked and she indicated using her fingers – great.

When you are cutting hair there is a consistency and even a sound to it that you become very familiar with, so when you cut something that isn't hair a horrible feeling shoots through you. That is what happened to me. I was pretty sure that what I had just snipped wasn't hair. There were no signs of blood, so that was a relief. It wasn't flesh, thank goodness! Any hairdresser who has had this happen will relate to what

I'm saying immediately. I searched around the lady's neck, combing the hair this way and that, but nothing.

I was puzzled and Linda sensed something was wrong. 'Is everything ok, Gordon?' she mouthed, so as not to draw attention. It's what hairdressers do.

'Yeah,' I shrugged my shoulders and continued combing. With no evidence of neck chains or the collar of her garment being snipped, I felt ok. I told myself it must have been a knot that I didn't quite comb free. All was good and Linda moved in and put the perm rods and lotion on the lady's head before moving her to the dryer.

When all the driers were occupied I sat down in the back of the shop with Linda and Irene, who worked with us, for a coffee and fag break. We'd often chat about the clients and any interesting conversations we'd had.

'What happened earlier, Gordon?' Irene asked. 'I saw Linda look at you and you looked a bit strange, was everything ok?' I smiled because I was relieved all over again and explained what had happened.

'Probably just a knot,' said Irene. 'Some of these old women have so much hairspray in their hair it takes ages tae get it oot.'

I was reassured, until I went to take the client from the drier to the backwash. 'Dae yae want tae come wae me, Mrs Johnson?' She just looked at me, but her absent expression told me that she hadn't heard a word I'd said. I leaned in close to her face. 'Mrs Johnson, let me take yae tae the sink!'

Linda had come out to the front of the shop.

'Huv yae turned yur hearing aid aff, Mrs Johnson? We ur taking yae through tae the sink noo, come own.' She turned to me then. 'They dae this these pensioners, they turn off the hearing aid to save the batteries.' I nodded in agreement as I got the woman onto the seat at the backwash basin and began to rinse the perm lotion from her rollered hair.

'These bloody cheap batteries, they're no worth tuppence near they ur, son.' The old lady banged at the battery pack in her cardigan pocket for a moment. I agreed with her, and continued to spray water over her head.

Her perm turned out great, though, and I didn't think any more of her hearing problem until I put her coat on her and walked her to the door. Still nothing seemed to be out of the ordinary until I looked at Linda. Her eyes were wide and stunned. I followed her look and my eyebrows could have shot off my head when I saw a long, beige wire trailing from below the old woman's coat as she exited the salon. I had a sudden realization of what the hard-knotted thing was that I had cut through at the back of her neck. It was, of course, the wire that connected her earpiece to the battery pack – which is how hearing aids used to be. None of us had the guts to tell the poor woman. Instead we all just stood there frozen as she left the salon mumbling to herself and hitting the pack with her hand repeatedly: 'Stupid fucking batteries, I should take them back tae that bloody shop.'

***

Paul was almost a year old when Katie and I decided to get married. It was March 1982. We didn't have a lot of money, but with my extra earnings from the homers, we were getting by. Katie and Josie also thought that it was right that we should marry rather than just live together. Katie felt it would be better for our son as he grew up. She was right, I suppose, but getting married on a shoestring is never a classy affair and if things that happen on the day you get married are any indication of the future you will have, then ours was to be at the mercy of the elements.

On the day we were to be married in the registry office in Martha Street in Glasgow, Katie wouldn't let me do her hair. Instead she asked me to give her a mousse she could put through it that would brighten it and lift the blonde colour. I told her the mousse she was looking for was already in the bathroom and that she should use the silver can as there were two different ones.

'Gordon, is this stuff supposed to be red?' Sometimes, blonde elements in tints and rinses are extreme colours, like blue or purple when they go on, but they wash out and leave only a warmth of tone, but this didn't sound right.

'Did you use the silver tin?' I asked from the other side of the bathroom door. There was a silence for a moment and then the door unlocked and slowly opened with my bride-to-be facing me with wet, but very noticeably burgundy hair. That might not have been so bad, but I knew that wet hair looks very different in colour from the tone it will dry out to be – and this reeked of pink. Katie had long thick, curly hair and she had put so much mousse on that it covered every last strand. Also because she had lots of bleached highlights, which are very porous, her hair had absorbed the pigment and developed to a bright pink shade that was not going to wash out for a long time. Her choices were to have her hair cropped to half an inch, or long, thick, curly and pink!

On hearing this dilemma, my mother came up with a great solution. Buy a hat. Not bad Lizzy, but we were skint at the time. Not one to be put off that easily my mother suggested buying a hat for a day, keeping the price tag on it and returning it the following morning to get a refund. It was a plan and better than the pinkish, punkish look that Katie was sporting at that moment. So a pink, wide brimmed hat was procured from the C&A department store in Argyll Street complete with its £10.99 price tag dangling from the inside. I put Katie's hair into a roll and the offending pink mass was tucked neatly under the hat along with the price tag. Lizzy looked very pleased with herself.

When it comes to the weather, March in Glasgow is rarely calm. Just as we came out of the registry office as man and wife, a huge gust of wind lifted the hat right off the head of the bride. It hovered above us for about five seconds before blowing straight into the nearest puddle. Katie let out a scream and I ran to get to the hat, but by that time it had absorbed half of the puddle and the cardboard price tag had turned to an inky grey as it floated out wide of the hat. I turned to Katie ready with a look of disappointment. But when I saw her hair had been blown free of the kirby grips and now resembled a bright pink mop of candyfloss, I spluttered and then burst out laughing too. Thank God we couldn't afford a photographer. Katie shrieked with laughter, and soon the small wedding party gathered on the windy Glasgow street, joined in. We were off to a rosy start. A bright pink, rosy start to be exact.

I soon realized that I could make much more money from being a self-employed mobile hairdresser around Springburn than the fiver a day Linda was paying me. For the next couple of years I built up quite a clientele for myself. I worked in people's homes and they would ask friends and family from all around. I was fast becoming known in North Glasgow.

Whenever Katie and I went to one of the local pubs, I could count on one hand the number of people who didn't have their hair styled by me. So before long I was able to save some money.

Our little flat was looking very smart. We seemed to keep up with the latest fashions in furnishings and décor and Katie always kept it spotless. My mother would be proud, you would think. Once a week, Lizzy would announce that she was coming to visit us. Four of her family still lived in the area and we were all on high alert when the call came that Lizzy was on her way. My sister Betty now lived closest to where mother got off the bus, so this meant she would go to hers first. Betty had moved from her little room and kitchen flat to a bigger two-bedroom flat like ours.

After leaving Betty, Lizzy might head to Jonny, who now lived with his girlfriend and their first son John, about ten minutes walk from my house. So we would be next, or it could be Joan who lived one minute from us. The thing was, we didn't always know how Lizzy's visits would go because it changed each week. We all believed she did this to catch someone out with an untidy house. The penalty for which was unthinkable.

We shouldn't have worried, because Katie was meticulous. But no matter how good it was, Old Lizzy would always find something. Even if the baby had just dropped a crumb on the floor, she would rush to pick it up and make mention of it. 'Look at that Katie, that baby has left crumbs there, ah mean if you don't get them up right away they might get trampled into your carpet. These things cause diseases and infections, ah hope yae watch fur this. There nothing worse than a dirty fucking hoos.' This kind of comment would get right on Katie's nerves, but most times she would bite her tongue and put up with the rant. 'Ah mean, yur wee hoos is looking clean and quite tidy ah suppose. Dae yae keep it like this awe the time?' By this point Katie would be on the point of exploding, so I would try to distract my mother. 'How was Betty and Jim then Ma, they ok?'

Lizzy would make a face like somebody just offended her. 'They think am daft, but they were jest oot ah thur bed two minutes before ah came in. Ah noticed newspapers pushed under cushions.'

I think that Katie and my mother got on pretty well. My mother sort of respected my wife because she was very clean and this was something my mother thought a wife should be. Also Katie wasn't in any way intimidated by her and, though she kept quiet during weekly inspections, she wouldn't always let my mother get the last word when it came to me or Paul.

One night while we were visiting my parents with Paul, the two women in my life had a kind of stand-off. It ended with me getting a punch in the ribs. My mother was very controlling when it came to her family. But Katie was, and always has been, quite a fiery person who will never back down when forced into a corner. I honestly don't remember how the argument began and neither can Katie, but it was probably over our son or me.

I was in one of the bedrooms with my dad and Paul. We were looking at old photos my dad had of his parents, when we heard raised voices in the living room. We both hurried along the hall to find my mother and Katie standing in the middle of the floor, both looking ready for a fight. So, naturally, I stood between them asking what the hell was going on.

Then Katie spoke at my mother over my right shoulder. 'Look Lizzy, you're too auld ah widnay fight wae yae. But ah wont let yae get away wae telling me how tae run my life. Your too auld anywae.' My mother spoke quietly and I knew that wasn't good. 'Is that right Katie?' She looked like she was stepping back and tensions relaxed for the moment.

Then my dad spoke to my mother. 'Sit doon and just hold your tongue. They're young so don't interfere, dae yae hear me?' She didn't say another thing but fired a fast, right jab towards Katie. I moved my body to block it and it caught me right in the ribs. I can assure you I was glad it caught me and not my wife. My ribs ached for days after that shot.

In the end, there was no great falling out between the two women. As I say, if anything, my mother liked Katie for being a strong person. In fact, she loved her company so much that she had a little surprise for us when she came on one of her weekly inspections. Katie and I had managed to save enough money to go on our first holiday abroad, so imagine our shock when Lizzy announced, 'You'll never guess what I've just done Katie? I jest booked the same holiday as you two in the same hotel and everything. Wit dae yae think awe that then?'

I wouldn't want to put into words what we thought of that. But this wasn't all. Katie's parents, who had just sold their small flat, decided that they would treat themselves to a wee holiday and join us too. This wasn't the worst thing because Josie loved to look after her only grandson and at least that meant that Katie and might get a night or two out. But the thought of my mother coming with us though . . . Well, everything we thought might happen did, and more. Much more.

None of us had flown before and that was a nightmare. My mother sat between Katie and me and spoke constantly about the plane crashing: 'Ah don't know Katie, this fucking thing could drap oot the sky at any minute am telling yae. Ah don't trust that driver. Ay wiz only young, did yae see him? He hud a right wee head, ay canny huv a lot a fucking brains?' Thankfully it was only a three hour flight to Palma. Any longer and I might have tried to crash the plane myself.

The hotel wasn't clean enough, so she found a shop that sold cleaning things and gave the room a once over. 'That's better. Yae don't know where these filthy Spanish bastards have been. Did yae see the dirt under her fucking nails? Honestly Katie, yae don't know where these filthy bastards have been.'

The food was not right either. Lizzy seemed to have a thing against Spanish anything. 'Ah bet they Spanish chickens are unclean. Naw, a widnay touch that and Ah canny eat the salad because they use that scabby fucking water or theirs to wash it. I'll huv a boiled egg.' I don't know if it was out of devilment, but Katie reminded her that the egg came out of the dirty Spanish chicken. So Lizzy had cheese and assumed that the cows in Spain were British. It took my mother several days to realize that the food on our buffet was ok. It had been well prepared and was clean, but she was definitely out of her comfort zone here.

My mother loved a bargain and you have no idea how she rejoiced when she bought sun cream for fifty pesetas from a bargain bin in one of the gift shops.

'That's great, what a bargain,' Josie told her. 'Wits it called Lizzy, what make is it?' My mother took off her glasses to get a better look at the writing, something I never understood throughout my life.

'Naw, ah canny read it, Josie. It's awe in Spanish. But they live here, they must know the good wans, ah imagine?' Well, she and my father dowsed themselves in the cheap Spanish cream while the rest of us got Nivea'd up to lie in the sun by the hotel swimming pool. It wasn't excruciatingly hot, but after a while we all went in for a break.

Katie drew my attention to something. 'Gordon, is it just me, or dae yur Ma and Da look awful broon?' They did, and my mother couldn't help point out how her bargain cream was a find, she just had to rub it in, as it were. It must have been an hour later when my father came into the room to get something that I noticed he was looking like Ray Charles. And not just because he was wearing sunglasses. His tan was still developing and he was now looking like he had changed race.

'Dad, have you seen yourself?' I asked him, and he looked in the mirror. I think the penny was begging to drop when the other half of the Motown tribute act entered the room.

'The sun must be fucking different oot here, Sammy,' she said. 'Look at the colour of us two.' I think you know what happened after shower time. 'Dirty fucking Spanish cheap, shite cream. Sammy, am white again!' We could hear her shouts through the thin walls of the cheap Spanish hotel and we laughed so loudly, it made our trip.

Another day, we were all sunbathing on loungers around the pool. Other holidaymakers were ranged round the other sides of the pool, kids were splashing happily in the shallow end, music was blaring out from an open window in the hotel. Out of the corner of my eye I noticed a woman on the other side light up a cigarette, and I sensed Lizzy was watching her too, as I felt her tense up.

'Look at that fucking whoor, Gordon. No, don't look!'

I looked. The woman with the cigarette, short brown hair, middle-aged and mumsy-looking was sunbathing topless.

'There's fucking kids here. It's fucking disgusting.'

'Mother, let it go.'

But at that moment the woman stood up, stretched her arms out to the side and arched her neck backwards, limbering up for a dive. Lizzy could contain herself no longer.

'Oh, the bastard's parading herself!' Before I could say anything she'd shot off her lounger, around the side of the pool and sort of rugby-tackled the woman, propelling her into the pool, arms, legs and tits flying everywhere. When she resurfaced Lizzy was standing over her on the edge of the pool shouting down at her: 'Yer midden, yer disgusting filthy whoor, cover yerself up!'

Lizzy came and plumped herself down on the sun lounger again with a grunt. 'Come on, Lizzy,' dad said clearing his throat. 'Let's get our things and go inside.'

Well, I suppose there is truth in that old saying, 'You can take the girl out of the Gorbals, but you can't take the Gorbals out of the girl.'

I could write a script about that holiday. A group of Glaswegians on a trip to Spain for the first time. But the one story that sums up this trip was on the flight home when Lizzy got involved in an on-board scrap.

Waiting to board the flight for our homeward journey my mother noticed a couple kissing in the departure lounge. 'Look at that hoor wae that auld man. Dirty, disgusting slut! Look at the wae she's dressed. Yae can see everything, cows like that turn ma stomach.' I think we can say she wasn't happy at the couple, who had a slight generation gap between them. Thankfully mother got diverted by other people who annoyed her. All was relatively well until we got into the air. After a short while she began to let us know again that we could all die if the engines stopped or we ran out of fuel. But then out of the side of my eye I saw something happening in the seats several rows behind us.

'Oh my god is that ah fight?' said one of the passengers.

'It's a fucking fight! Watch Katie let me oot.' Mother was out of her seat like a greyhound out of the traps. She saw a woman pummelling the older man from the check-in, and in a second she was grabbing the woman by the shoulders and shaking her. 'Hit an alud man wull yae?' Lizzy was ready for a real go now. A steward grabbed my mother and pulled her out of the way. The woman Lizzy was restraining fought free and went back to pummelling the old man. Only now it became clear that she was attempting to revive the guy, who'd had a heart attack. The stewardess who was doing this was also trying to get an oxygen mask from the panel above over his face, while his girlfriend was becoming hysterical next to him.

'See a knew something bad would come oot owe that, she wiz far too young fur that poor auld bastard, Katie, did ah no say that?'

Can you imagine the relief we felt when that plane landed in Glasgow? What was more, Lizzy changed her tune about the young woman as she was leaving the plane with her partner, helping him to a waiting ambulance. 'God help hur, that poor lassie. She's no as young as ah first thought she wiz. Wae awe that sobbing her face looks bloated and yae can see her real age. Auch, God help her, ah hope it didn't ruin her wee holiday.'

Katie and I swore we would never go on holiday with my parents again after that. We did. Three more times, and each one was worse and more hectic than the one before it. I say this, but the laughs that we still get remembering those madcap trips, give us hours of great stories to tell – even if it wasn't quite so funny living through it. My mother gave us many such memories.

Katie got pregnant again on that first holiday. I actually knew when my son Steven was conceived. Something like an electric shock went through my body, telling me that my wife would be pregnant. (Later Katie made the comment, 'Yae weren't that good, son.') Several weeks later she duly told me she was pregnant. Checking back her dates to the middle of January when we were in Spain, she concluded that I might have been right.

It was a very different experience for us when Katie was pregnant for the second time. I was only twenty-one and would be twenty-two when my son was born, but I didn't feel like the little boy lost that I did when she was carrying Paul.

The summer of 1984 was hot in Glasgow and the pregnancy was quite uncomfortable. Katie looked exhausted by the time we got through to October when she was due. I attended the birth of my second child, something I hadn't been able to bring myself to do when Paul was born. My second son arrived on the afternoon of 9 October 1984. He weighed in at eight pounds and six ounces and was very healthy in every way. From the moment he was born we had a connection. Maybe we had a connection even before that.

When Steven was a newborn, I was around the house much more and was able to watch him and spend time with him. Paul had the routine of going to his Grandad-Joe, as he called him, and Josie would often take him to stay with her on weekends, so we were used to Paul being passed around the family. But Steven was instantly attached to me. I was a more relaxed parent the second time around, which I'm sure he benefitted from.

My Uncle Barney, diagnosed with lung cancer back in 1970, was now told that he had six months to live, but he was still going strong and his sense of humour hadn't given way either. We were all sure that's what kept him going.

He always said that he wasn't fond of children, but his bark was always worse than his bite. The moment he saw Paul he was smitten. It was hard not to be. At the age of three my son could read and would often pick up the newspaper and read out the headlines. Barney loved this. He encouraged Paul to read aloud from different books and magazines around his home. He was also amazed at how clearly my son spoke to adults. Not like a child, but more like a grown-up. 'Barney, this pen that is made of metal must be your best pen I would say, so, can I borrow one of the others to write with please?' My uncle would roar with laughter.

I was often amazed at how well-turned-out our kids were considering how much I earned, and how we always seemed to be buying the latest things. We had hi-fi systems, hi-tech video and TV equipment and in our bedroom we had this really swish, five-door wardrobe with sets of matching draws. All our carpets had been changed to much better quality. I should have done the maths.

'How did you manage to buy that stuff Katie?'

'I got the bedroom stuff from a woman roon the corner who has split wae her man. She gave us it fur next tae nothing. She's moving away and the video, ma ma bought us that. The rest came from the money you gave me.' It felt good, I must say. But my father always used to say, 'If something looks too good to be true, it's usually because it is.'

It was at this time I got a call out of the blue from my Aunt Sylvia, asking if I would bring Katie and the children to see her. We'd been planning to go to London to visit my Uncle Barney with Paul, so we said we would travel over from north London where he lived to Sutton and spend the day with her. This pleased her no end. I felt a little strange about it because she hadn't really shown any interest in my new family to this point and, though I was excited for them to meet her, and experience something of a part of my life that had been so special, it left me feeling awkward at best.

We were only with Aunt Sylvia and Uncle Michael one day, but I think my aunt spent at least a hundred pounds on clothes and toys for him and Steven. Like any child, Paul was in heaven, in much the same way I had been when I had met this lovely lady as a small boy.

Katie told me that the way my aunt looked at Paul made her feel so sorry for the woman. She believed that Sylvia was wondering what her grandchild would have looked like had her son lived. Stephen would have been my age. But it was great to have my aunt and uncle back in my life and also in the lives of my sons, who seemed to be growing faster than we could imagine. For Paul his Great Aunt Sylvia was the best person he had ever met in his life. To prove that when he got back to Glasgow he showed everyone the dickey bow that she bought for him. Strange child. Of all the things he could have asked for, he asked for this.

Paul had only just started primary school when his teacher sent for us. I remember worrying. Paul was never trouble, never displayed any bad temper as a child, so what could this be about? I was a little surprised when the teacher said, 'Are you aware of how well your son can read for his age?' Well, of course we were. Every night my son would read himself to sleep. The problem for the school was that Paul was ahead of all the other children. They weren't sure what to do with him or how to progress and wondered if we might have any suggestions. That was when Paul started on his own little projects, based on trips we would take together on weekends to museums and places of interest, of which Glasgow has many. These projects became his extra school work which he did until the other kids caught up.

Both my sons enjoyed it when I took them on field trips to castles. Sometimes I'd take them to the gymnastics camp where the Scottish team trained. I still knew all the coaches. Steven loved to play around on the apparatus, while Paul sat in a corner with his nose in a book. My boys were growing up nicely, they were doing ok, and all seemed to be well.

Around the same time I was offered a job in a new salon that was opening up in our area. The owner thought I would bring a lot of business to the shop and she paid me enough to enable me to give up most of my homers. The shop, called Top Edge, was at the top of Edgefauld Road right next door to where my sister Betty lived. Another stylist was brought in, a young woman called Christine Peebles. She lived in the flat above Katie's mother and she and Katie had long been friends. Christine told me that Katie had had a crush on her older brother Brian when they were growing up.

The job turned out well for me because I could walk to

the salon in five minutes, and work regular nine-to-five hours again. It was brilliant to have much more time at home.

Christine and I worked in Top Edge for almost two years together, until I was asked by one of my clients if I would go over to the local pub called the Morven and meet with a guy called Jimmy who had a proposal for me. I had no idea what this could be about, but I told Christine and she said I should go, just to find out.

It turned out that Jimmy Mackintosh wanted to give me a chance to run a salon for him in Possil Park, a fifteen minute drive from where I lived. He offered me more money than I was getting and what's more, he wanted Christine to come with me. Apparently people liked the way we worked and saw how we had built up a big clientele between us. Jimmy, who already had several salons, wanted to poach us.

Katie and I had many discussions about this change, including with Christine and her then boyfriend Robert. We'd been doing ok and were worried about making the change. Possil Park had a real reputation for junkies, a term which wasn't so familiar back then. But we decided that we were from Springburn, which wasn't much different, and in the end, the idea of being our own bosses and earning more money swayed us. A month later we had moved into the little salon on Saracen Street, the main street running through the centre of Possil Park. We called it New Image.

You know how some things in your life cause you concern, but the pull to go towards them is greater than your fear? That was what it felt like for both Christine and me at the time. The day we walked into this small salon, which was clean and bright as hairdressers go, it was different. It was different because we had stepped out of what we knew and were safe in. We'd gone out on a limb and taken a chance on something unknown. I now believe that such moments in life are presented to us so that our futures can be changed by that one decision, there and then. Somehow mine and Christine's lives became entwined.

My goodness, the people of Possil were like characters from the old Gorbals! The first day we opened for trade we were told by one woman that the previous staff had fleeced her for quite a large sum of money. Someone else told us never to let Christine walk along the street on her own or she might get raped. Strangely no one thought to warn me of such things. Our eyes were opened completely at midday on the day we opened the door to our business, when a nineteen year old girl fell unconscious in the doorway of our shop. Apparently she had taken a cocktail of drugs and by the time an ambulance came she was already dead. I remember that Christine and I went to help this young woman, which is the natural thing to do, until a police constable rushed over and told us, 'Don't touch her, she's a wee junky and she might have AIDS.' What? We didn't have AIDS in our world just fifteen minutes away and neither of us had really seen a junky, let alone watched one die in front of us. I think I can speak for my colleague when I say. 'What the f—k had we done?'

If all that occurred on our first day was an indication of things to come, we had two choices. The first was to pack our things and head back to Springburn and beg for our old jobs back. The second was to adapt and go with it and see what would come next. I must say that for all it seemed crazy, there was something else going on here that intrigued us. Who knows, maybe it was the in-your-face attitude of the place and its hard reality check. But we both agreed. We were staying.

11

Deep Debt–Latent Power

My son Steven had just had his second birthday. One Sunday afternoon I was showing him off in my mother's home. His hair was so blonde it was almost white, emphasizing his big round blue eyes, which flashed at all the family when they played with him or picked him up. 'Gordon, he's your double when you were that age,' Betty said as she lifted my son above her head and jiggled him playfully.

Everybody in our family seemed to be in my parents' high rise flat in Norfolk Court this day. My brother Tommy was there with his new wife Marry, as was Sammy who was now married to Maureen. They had a daughter called Donna whose hair was as black as Steven's was blonde. Donna and her mother were Spanish-looking. Jonny was also there that day with his two boys John and Andrew and to round things off, Joan arrived with her twin boys and her youngest daughter Karen.

'Fur fuck sake, this hoos is like a menagerie wae awe these waens,' Lizzy called out, sounding exasperated.

'Ma, Sauchiehall Street's not as busy as this!' Tommy shouted back at her above the rabble.

'Well ah might go there tae get some fucking peace and quiet next week,' Lizzy shouted back. Our family was expanding, but Lizzy was right there at the centre of it and still true to form.

Each weekday morning bar one, a Wednesday, which was my day off from the salon, I picked Christine up from the flat she was sharing with her older brother Brian and drove her to work. We now had another member of staff called Tricia, who fitted in really well with us. Possil Park seemed to suit us. The people here had lives to talk about and get involved with.

All hairdressers become connected to the community they work in. For many people going to the hairdresser is like going to the confessional, and if you work in a salon you learn to become a great listener, hearing about people's troubles and their pain. Some people even called us their fourth emergency service. Working as a barber and a hairdresser was great training for my life's work helping people to cope with grief and bereavement.

As hard and tough and chaotic as Possil Park was as a place, Christine and I agreed it had soul and we wanted to be part of it. I remember talking to a woman called Wee Maggie while perming her hair. Her grandson was only twenty and he was a junky living, begging and stealing out on the streets. This was a young man who just two years previously had been about to sign a deal with Glasgow Rangers, to train with them and hopefully play first team football. This should have been his life, only one Saturday night before the contract signing, he went to a party with his friends and, though he didn't have any interest in taking drugs before this, Wee Maggie said that someone from the neighbourhood persuaded him to try some. Now a zombie was all that was left of her once handsome, happy grandson, and his bright future had been stolen by some uncaring drug dealer.

Wee Maggie wasn't done, though. She was just one of the many in the area who were trying to get together and fight for Possil's young people. She was a woman in her late sixties, whose husband had died of alcoholism, but she wasn't beaten. She was trying to raise awareness of the effects of drink and drugs in her community. To us, Maggie represented the other face of the people of this place, those who were caring and determined and surely put here for a bigger purpose.

Shoplifting was the local sport of junkies, we decided, because every day our door would burst open with two or three women, either drugged off their faces or gagging for their next hit. Either way, it didn't look pretty. 'Anybody want tae buy a size fourteen dress oot ah Marks? It sells fur twenty-five quid in the shop, but we're daen it fur a tenner. Ok, a fiver then, any takers?' Dresses were one thing, but we even had guys walk in to the salon asking if we wanted to buy a fridge-freezer and other white goods. After a while, we didn't even try to work out how they got them out of the stores. It's fair to say that while working at New Image, there was never a dull moment – but that also meant that you could never let your guard down for a second.

There was also a drugs problem growing in our own area now around Drumbottie Road. Some of the kids we'd watched grow up for the last few years, children of family friends, were rumoured to be using.

Yes, we had seen glue sniffing and underage drinking, but this was a whole new other level – needles and the hard stuff.

I remember I had a great urge to buy a flat and get out of Springburn. I knew that if I could save enough money for the deposit it would give us more choice, rather than be trapped in the type of place that the council could offer us. I wanted to move to somewhere a little less chaotic where the street wasn't so open to all and sundry. We were finding it increasingly hard to keep track of all the different people walking through the entrance to our flats. Kids into drugs in our street were bringing people in from Possil and other areas where drugs were more common. I think Katie and I knew we'd had enough when Paul, only about five years old, pointed to a used syringe and needle that had been left lying on a step behind where we lived. It was time to get our kids out of there.

The bible tells us 'seek and ye shall find'. I wasn't really looking for answers on a biblical scale, but during my quest to find a screwdriver to fix some drawers that had come loose in our bedroom, I happened upon the answer to why our house looked so good and how my sons were the best turned-out in our street.

I remember being at home alone one Sunday morning while Katie was out with the boys when I noticed that the bottom drawer of one of our units was sitting askew. I'm no perfectionist when it comes to this stuff, but something urged me to put it right again. When I tried to push the drawer back to its closed position it came up against some resistance. I pulled the drawer all the way out. 'What the hell can be trapped under there?' I spoke to the empty room. I put my hand into the space and found that it was bulging with papers. Taking them out a bit at a time I noticed that they were mostly envelopes. In fact, they all looked like bills and there were some scraps of paper with figures written on them.

On closer inspection I found out that we were in lots of debt. I had thought that we were doing well. I was earning more than enough now to pay for the things we needed. But most of these bills and demands were two, even three years old, for furniture that Katie had told me she'd sold because someone offered her as much as she paid for it. It meant that we could have the latest thing. Well, that's how Katie had sold it to me. I was shocked. I couldn't work it out because, though Katie spent lots on the kids and our home, she never really spent it on herself. So where was all this money? I needed answers.

Katie is the worst liar in the world. When she came back to the flat I told her that I'd fixed the drawer. She looked at me for a second wondering, I imagined, if her stash had been found, but I didn't give anything away.

'Oh good,' she said. 'Ah think we'll get new drawers for that room, maybe even a whole new set. There's these mirrored ones that are oot noo that look brilliant. Angie next door just got them . . .'

I wanted to let her continue to see if she would tell me about all the letters and the unpaid bills that had built up, but she just carried on like nothing was out of place.

'Dae yae think we can *afford* a new bedroom unit Katie?'

She looked at me very seriously for a moment before she answered, and I thought I saw a look of admission take over, but no. 'Well, ah was gonnay tell yae. Ah think I'll get a wee job noo that Steven's aboot tae go to nursery. Jest fur a couple of hours. I'll buy the new wardrobes and things. Ah mean, we've nay debt noo or anything, so ah might even get it on hire purchase. Whit dae yae think?'

'Hire purchase? We've always just bought things when we could afford it, or when your grandad lent us the money. Why would we want to get hire purchase, Katie?'

'Yae know, I have tae run roon tae ma mother's fur a wee minute, I'll be back soon. We'll talk aboot it then.' She must have had an idea that I had found the bills and all the debt letters and needed time to think. How could I have been so stupid? I looked around at our flat and realized that nothing belonged to us.

Katie came back into the flat, all guns blazing. 'Right noo, before yae start judging me, cause ah know that you've found the debt letters, can ah jest say that it wisnay me that used the money. Lots of people owe *me* money, well us ah mean. But I'll get some of it back soon . . .' It went on and on, but the upshot was that Katie had helped her mother and aunt and some of our neighbours to pay rent when they were completely skint. It had all seemed to pile up. Rather than tell me, she decided to play catch up. She told the people sending the demands that the money would be paid next month and then the next and eventually she stopped telling them anything.

My heart sank. All my hopes of getting a small mortgage to move my family were dashed. I wanted to go to my father, but I didn't want him to think I was a failure. I plucked up the courage to go to the rent place and the debt people and talk to them about repayment plans. I must admit that if you ever want to feel lower than a nursing ant's tit, sit in front of people who you owe money to and let them reprimand you.

After about ten meetings in one week I actually got good at it, and before I knew, it didn't hurt anymore. I almost took a loan from one company, who felt so sorry for me, they said that they were willing to consolidate all my debts into one big loan at a million per cent interest or something. I decided I needed to take back the control from these people who basically were little petty dictators. They felt powerful when dealing with people on low incomes like us, who need to borrow just to have a half decent standard of living. Instead of getting down, I decided to tackle the problem head on. I went out doing as many homers as I could to get enough money to pay all the debts. I think I was living on fumes. I was getting home so late that the boys were asleep and then going out in the morning and running the salon. But discovering Katie's stash of debt letters had been a blessing in disguise, because I now knew I needed to run the finances.

Katie was very quiet for the next while and I noticed that none of our furniture changed during this period. As far as clothing the boys went, I told her she should take up knitting. She did funnily enough, but her talents would have been better served in the Middle Ages as most of the garments she made looked like chainmail.

There was one night around this time that I will never forget. In fact, it was Tuesday 8 March 1987. I had finished my work in the salon and felt relaxed because I was to have a day off the following day. I handed the keys over to Christine, who opened up the salon on Wednesdays. She was happy and excited because she and her brother and one of his friends had just bought a flat in the trendy west end of Glasgow. They were in that fun phase of making the place their own. Also she was meeting her brother later in a pub in town. Brian worked in one of the big theatres in the centre of Glasgow and they often went with the crew for drinks after performances. Christine liked the buzz. All in all, it was a night that I remember because of the good feeling we both had as we left the salon and locked up.

I watched a Steve Martin movie on television that night, *The Man with Two Brains*. I remember this because I videoed it for Christine because she was going out. I went to bed at a normal time, which would be just before midnight as I always sat up late back then. I dropped off to sleep at once.

I was dreaming and yet the quality of this dream made it feel very real. There were people in a street who I didn't know, but yet somehow I did. I was in Glasgow somewhere and I was aware there was a strange blue tone to the light around me. There was another person there standing behind me but my head wouldn't turn so I couldn't see who it was. Then there was a silence that was different from any silence I had ever known. No, I had felt this silence once before when I was a boy, but it didn't matter. I liked this warm feeling like I was inside a bubble or something . . . Then suddenly I woke up and was looking at Brian Peebles, Christine's brother. He was standing in our bedroom directly in front of me and I was sitting up in my bed.

Brian looked good. His face was alive with something, an energy maybe, I couldn't tell. But he was smiling, not a gushy smile, but a knowing smile and I felt happy for him. He was wearing a tartan shirt with his sleeves rolled up to his elbows and tight denim jeans. I remember this because I recall that I could only see him from the knees up and just as I had that thought, he disappeared through the floor of my bedroom.

I wasn't scared in the least by this vision of my friend's brother standing in my bedroom while Katie lay sleeping by my side, but the moment he vanished my heart began to beat like a drum. In my mind's eye, I could see people walking towards me. My eyes were wide open now, but the people were still there, like a kind of hologram in the distance. I could see them clearly even though they were miles away. My instinct made me turn and hit the switch on the clock radio beside me. I saw the numbers on the clock flashing 6.30am and heard a man's voice blaring out at me, 'A fire has swept through a home in the west end of Glasgow.'

Katie sat up beside me. 'What is it, is something wrong?' I didn't answer her because in my vision I saw two police officers walking towards our front door and I jumped out of bed. There is no way I could actually have seen the officers coming towards our flat from my bedroom. To do that I would have had to see through three walls . . .

There was a very loud knock at our front door but I was already standing behind it waiting to open it to the police.

'Gordon Smith, are you Gordon Smith?'

'Yes.' This was all I could manage to say. I remember just staring at them.

'There's been an accident and I have been asked to pass these keys on to you by Miss Christine Peebles.' The officer looked blank.

'Is she ok?' I asked, my heart pounding by this time. The police were reluctant to go into it, but then Katie came up behind me saying that it had been reported on the radio there had been a fire in Buckingham Terrace. Her words shot through me because that was the street where Christine and Brian had moved to and I *knew* it was their flat.

I got myself dressed and headed for the shop. There I made calls to a couple of Christine's friends and soon discovered that the fire had been in her flat, but that she was ok and with a friend. She had been sedated. There were still reports coming on the news saying about the fire and that one person had died. No names were given. An hour or so later Brian's name was announced as the one who had perished in the house fire in Buckingham Terrace in the early hours of that morning.

People have asked me since, why I didn't tell Christine about the vision I had of her brother the morning he died. The reality was that after the news of his death, it was not upper-most in my thoughts. My only concern was how could I help my friend. As a teenager Christine had lost her mother in very tragic circumstances and she hadn't had the greatest relationship with her father since then. She would need all the support she could get.

Brian's funeral took place on the following Saturday and I made the offer to my friend that people do. 'Christine, if there is anything I can do for you, please . . .'

I didn't get to finish what I was saying as she grabbed my arm tightly and with the most intense look on her face she demanded, 'Take me to a Spiritualist church, I need to see a medium.'

I didn't try to question what she said. Instead I nodded my head and whispered to her, 'Ok.'

Christine later said that it had been out of pure desperation that she had asked me to take her to a Spiritualist church. None of us even knew where we would find such a place. They didn't exactly advertise themselves. But later that day, Christine came to me again and in all seriousness repeated the request. Now, this was strange when I think back because she wasn't actually asking for a medium, which might have conjured up images of séances and creepy stuff, but for a church. I promised that I would help and by the end of the day I had found out that there were several Spiritualist churches in Glasgow. Through the grapevine that is hair-dressing, I discovered that a famous medium was attending the biggest church the following evening.

Against many people's wishes I took Christine and Brian's girlfriend Fiona to Somerset Place, where the Glasgow Association of Spiritualists held services three times a week. This Victorian hall had a wrought iron staircase ascending to another level in the corner and about two hundred seats facing a low, shallow stage with a curtain at the back. It was bare apart from a banner with the slogan 'Nature, Truth and Light!' On this Sunday the visiting medium was a woman from Edinburgh called Mary Duffy. When people in the congregation even just mentioned her name I could sense excitement.

I had it all worked out. There would be people planted in the audience and the old con woman would just talk general claptrap. Very needy people would then cling on to whatever she suggested because it was what they wanted to hear.

But I was surprised by Mrs Duffy. She came out onto the platform and spoke in a very intelligent fashion about how the whole business of mediumship worked. She was neither patronizing, nor did she seem like a con artist. This very nice, open and sincere woman was evidently not trying to take people in. The way she spoke sounded kind and giving. I looked at Christine and Fiona who did seem to be hanging on to every word, and I tried to remain objective. That is, until she turned her attention directly to us.

'May I speak to the young woman at the front on this side, please?' The three of us might as well have been hit with a stun gun, because none of us was ever going to speak in front of this crowd of about two hundred and fifty people. 'Darling, can I just hear your voice and then I can work with you?' Again, none of us flinched. Mrs Duffy then looked directly at Christine and said, with the most caring of expressions on her face, 'Darling, you wouldn't have to be a medium to know that you have just suffered a terrible loss. So let me just say that I will speak to you later in private, if I may. Only your mother wants you to know that she has him with her . . .' The medium looked like she was conducting a conversation with an invisible person beside her and I noticed a light around her that was like the light from the sun. Of course I had seen light around people before, but never like this.

'Sweetheart, I don't want to do this in public and I'm sure you could do without this too, so we will speak later. But the young man here . . .' She pointed and I looked behind me, but there was no young man to be seen. Was this woman talking to me? As she focused her gaze on me, it was clear she was. 'Darling, does your friend know that you are a medium like me?' *Shut up crazy lady!* is what I wanted to say, but I sat rigid in my seat realizing that everyone was now focused on me. I could feel their eyes burning into my back as Mrs Duffy carried on: 'Yes, I have Sarah here with me. It's your grandmother, dear. Oh she's so proud of you and says you have sensed her presence before, is that right?' I don't think I replied, but I might have nodded. Oh my God, I was a closet medium being outed in public. 'Darling, your gran tells me that you will be standing where I am on this very platform five years from now. Oh my goodness, you have a lot of work to do for the spirit . . .' I wanted her to stop. Christine had turned to look at me with an expression of pure shock.

The service as a whole was quite amazing and compelling. This medium was coming out with people's exact names and even addresses, places and dates when people had died. When Mrs Duffy spoke to Christine and Fiona after the service I was even more impressed. She said that Brian would be at peace, with spirits looking after him, that his mother was with him and that it was time to grieve and then move on with life. She made it ok for them to miss him, but gave them re-assurance that he was still somehow consciously aware. It kind of made sense and she wasn't selling anything or trying to convert them to her religion. For me that made it ok.

'Excuse me young man, but are you developing your gift?' Ok, I liked this woman and what she said to my friend at this very sad time, but she really needed to back off.

'I'm sorry but I don't know what you're talking about. I'm not . . .'

She sort of dismissed me: 'Betty, who is running a good circle that we could get this young man into?' The word 'circle' immediately shot images of goats and virgins and black magic into my mind and I wasn't comfortable.

'Is this the one who was sitting at the front, Mary?' Betty Whitelaw was everything I thought a medium should look like. She had her steel grey hair tied in a bun and a white streak at the front that made her look as if she had had a fright. She spoke very kindly to my friends and then with no pressure, she handed me a piece of paper with a name and address written on it. 'If you ever get the feeling to follow up what Mary has said, I would recommend this person,' she said. 'She is very good at developing mediums. And don't look so worried, we only *look* mad, ha, ha, ha . . .' Then she walked away. I felt better when I heard her joke – it was hard not to like this woman. But then I thought for a second, shit, how did she know what I was thinking?

Our first visit to the Spiritualist church had been helpful. Just a week or so later, Christine made a decision to try to get back to a normal working life. I think more than anything, she needed work to keep her mind from constantly reliving the events of that night. What could they have done differently that would have meant her brother would still be alive?

We spoke about the medium. Mrs Duffy had spoken about Christine's mother being with HIM. Could she have just made this up at random? No, there were all the other messages that night. She never once repeated her information. Each person was given his or her individual message which fitted.

'What about your message?' Christine asked me. 'What was all that about, ah mean is your granny's name Sarah?' I had pondered a lot on all this, but I didn't want to burden Christine with it, she was so fragile at the time. I just said I would think about it.

My life was about to change again. Jimmy, who owned our salon, told me he was friendly with a financial advisor who would be able to get me a mortgage. He said that I should start to look for new places to live. I was delighted and scared at the same time. The thought of moving to a better area was amazing, but the idea of taking on a mortgage was terrifying. If only I knew then that this was all just part of growing up and becoming a proper parent.

But I was learning to face my fears in my life. After I had spoken with Katie about it, we made up our minds that we wanted to live in Dennistoun. This is a district about a mile from the High Street in Glasgow, near Alexandra Park. It would be good for the boys and quite close to town. But the great thing about the streets in this area was that everybody *owned* their homes. People chose to live there who wanted to better themselves and create something for their kids' futures.

A weight lifted from my shoulders the day we moved away from Drumbottie Road and headed for Garthland Drive in Dennistoun. We knew lots of good people from Springburn and glad to say, still do, but there was a desire for change inside me. I had to bring it to life. I had realized that I could force change in my life if I needed to, and I did not need to get stuck somewhere and be a victim of circumstance.

We bought our first flat for nineteen thousand pounds, more money than I could have imagined at the time. Our repayments were about forty pounds a month. Not as bad as I feared, and if I kept doing homers I could easily afford it. Also Steven would be starting school the following summer so Katie could go out to work more. She was already working in a café in Alexandra Parade just five minutes walk from the flat.

Paul settled in very well at his new school. His teacher reckoned he had the reading ability of an intelligent adult, and he was only six.

Though our new place was quieter and better for the children, people in the area didn't seem to speak to each other much. For Katie, it was a different world. There were no neighbours chatting to each other through open windows or on street corners. She had been brought up to visit her grandfather almost every day of her life; now she mainly contacted him by phone. The lack of other company meant we spent more time with each other, and started to argue. Our marriage was changing.

I went to several Sunday evening services at the Spiritualist church. Each time I did, a medium I'd never clapped eyes on, would start saying the same thing to me as Mary Duffy: 'Oh, are you a medium sir?' I would be given messages from my grandmother and once from my father's father, telling me again that I should go to a development class. I still hadn't taken it further, but neither had I thrown away the paper with the address. I began to read around the subject and found that there were arguments both for and against mediumship and spiritualism. I discovered that intelligent men like Arthur Conan Doyle and the physicist Sir William Crookes, both supported the idea of life after death, based on evidence they had observed. However, there was also an awful lot of criticism. There were mediums who staged séances producing puppets and other nonsense in darkened rooms. They'd pretend to be in a trance and talk in funny voices. And they charged people lots of money.

I decided to put out a challenge to any spirits who might want to prove to me that they actually existed. I wrote on a piece of paper the name of my grandmother's partner, Ummy and a question for him to answer me whenever he could. I wanted him to confirm that he had appeared to me as a child. Not another person in the world knew about my challenge. One Sunday evening out of the blue, Katie's friend Nina came to visit us in our new home. They obviously wanted me out of the way so they could talk, so I decided to go out to the Spiritualist church. However, because of a strange sequence of events, I didn't end up going to the one I knew.

As I was driving slowly along, about to turn right toward the church, a man waved me down. 'Excuse me, but can you tell me where the Spiritualist church in Berkeley Street is?' I was taken aback because people only whispered when they mentioned the Spiritualists in Glasgow. I had never heard anyone ask out loud in the street about it. I was about to tell him that the church he probably wanted was around the corner, and that I was going there, when he pressed a note into my hand. It had the address 64, Berkeley Street written on it. I realized that we were right in front of that very address as we spoke. As I pointed to the number 64 on the Georgian style house, I noticed a door open and some people came and stood outside and looked up and down the street. My intuition told me to get out of the car. As I stood next to the stranger, we both noticed a small plaque on the black metal railings. It read 'Spiritualist Church'.

I felt this was a sign of some kind and instead of going around the corner to Somerset Place, where I normally went, I entered number 64. It felt right. I listened to the same hymns and prayers that they had in the other church and then it was time for the medium. A woman called Mrs Hawthorn had come to give her demonstration of mediumship to the congregation. This lady was very different to Mary Duffy. In fact, she was nothing like any of the mediums I had seen so far. From the moment she opened her mouth, I thought Big Mary Hawthorn could have fitted in well with my own family.

'Hod own a wee minute wid yae,' she appeared to be arguing with the spirits. 'I've goat a wee man here wae a very funny name, but I'm trying tae get it right. Tummy, or Gummy? Oh for God sake tell me clearer wid yae?' I was speechless because I realized I was about to get the answer to my secret question. But also I knew this was Ummy trying to get through to this big awkward woman. I could feel it.

'Right, you.' She pointed directly at me. 'This wee man wae the funny name wants you tae know that yae did see him that dae. Hod own a wee minute,' she was arguing with him again. Then it came out of her mouth and she couldn't stop it, 'Ummy, Ummy, Ummy.' She said his name three times, but she looked so confused each time she said it. It was as if the spirit used her voice and not her brain.

'Yes,' I called out. 'I completely understand what you have just said.' She looked perplexed for a minute and then looked right into my soul.

'Good, then get yur arse roon tae the development circle and stop messing aboot wae tests.'

If I ever wanted evidence that the spirits were an intelligent force, this was it. Ummy was such an uncommon name and watching Mrs Hawthorn trying to make sense of it told me this wasn't coming from her, but from an external source. Ummy had answered my question. But the last part of the message, the bit about the development circle, I hadn't expected. Just before she finished, Mrs Hawthorn gave me one final message, 'We'll be there fur Barney, tell yur Ma.'

My Uncle Barney died later that week – I didn't tell my mother. I didn't think she would understand. But my mind was opening to so many new possibilities. All I could do was keep investigating. The next thing for me to do was to try this development circle and see if there was anything in it. The worst thing that could happen was I would waste a night of my life.

Christine asked me from time to time if I was going to the Spiritualist church. She felt she didn't need to go back and I was proud of her. She was still very brittle, but her strength was visible to those of us who knew her well. I knew now that Christine was going to be ok.

Katie and I didn't see too much of each other during this period. She was working more. Her mother, Josie, was living with us by then. She and Katie's stepfather Bob, had split and Josie was a bit lost. I think being close to Paul and Steven gave her a focus, but it probably put pressure on us too.

In fact, it often felt like there was a dark cloud beginning to settle over our family. Many things happen when you force change. Usually the most obvious are the things you *want* to see.

12

Opening Up

I was standing in the middle of West Princes Street in Glasgow, a street I had never been in before, looking around for the Spiritualist church. The piece of paper that Betty Whitelaw had given me on my first visit to the church on Somerset Place just read JEAN PRIMROSE, SPIRITUALIST CHURCH, WEST PRINCES STREET. That was it. No number or anything. I had walked the length of this street several times, but still there was nothing that looked like a church. Just as I was about to give up a small elderly woman with white set hair came out from behind a pair of large, black storm-doors and called out, 'Are you looking for me?' I looked at her and shrugged as I really had no idea who she was. But she motioned me towards her: 'Hurry up, come on we are about to start.'

Asking no questions, I followed this little woman. She ushered me through a hallway stacked with chairs into a larger, dimly lit room. About forty people were sitting in a wide circle around the edge of this room. They all stared at me as I was led to an empty seat. As my eyes adjusted, I tried to make out some of the faces, but the blurred red light made it almost impossible. 'Sit here close to me and just be quiet.'

Everyone closed their eyes as the white-haired woman opened the proceedings with a short prayer, addressing God and spirit. I could barely concentrate, let alone meditate, but I was intrigued to watch. Would spirits appear in the middle of the room? Or people levitate on chairs? My mind was racing with excitement, fear and pure wonderment.

After the prayer everyone went quiet. The old woman sat silently in her chair. Then she looked right at me and mouthed that I should close my eyes. I didn't want to, but followed her orders. Nothing happened for about ten minutes or so. Then just when I was drifting into semi-sleep, a man's voice boomed out, talking loudly in an Indian accent. 'Good evening Lady, Gentleman, deary, deary me!' My eyes were still shut but I could tell that the voice was coming from someone in the circle, in front of me and over the other side of the room. If this was supposed to be channelling, it sounded like a comedy sketch from the television. He said that the spirit world wants us to have a better understanding of how we treat our 'waens' – an odd Glaswegian-Indian mix. Then when this male voice stopped, there was a sound of a chair moving, as if someone else in the circle had stood up, and a woman started speaking with a Chinese accent. She started talking about love, saying something about how we will all enter the spirit world in a more elevated state if we love each other more in this life. I had kept my eyes firmly closed through all of this wisdom from on high, but now I decided to risk peeking at the priestess of Peking, who seemed to me somewhere over to my left. Strangely, my eyes wouldn't seem to open.

I drifted away from the room into a sort of dream and for a while I really lost touch with where I was. There was a sense of a light being switched on. Later I thought about waking up, but I decided to stay a bit longer. Eventually my eyes opened of their own accord in the dim, red-lit room full of strangers. It felt as though everyone was looking at me again as the old lady spoke softly, 'Are you ok, son?' I said 'Yes,' very quietly to her. Whatever had happened was over. I felt remarkably well.

It turned out that the old woman at the front of the room, was indeed the Mrs Primrose I had been looking for and that this was her little Spiritualist church. At the end of the meditation session she asked everyone in turn what they had experienced. Some went into long, complicated accounts of spiritual happenings that sounded totally bananas. 'I saw two Angels, one was Michael and the other Raphael and they took me on a journey into the heavens . . .' Others would say little, maybe just that they had a good meditation and felt better. I knew which group I belonged to. When the more extreme stories were being recounted, Mrs Primrose had a look on her face that suggested to me that she didn't believe them at all – but she evidently tolerated them. After all, where else were these people going to go?

As the circle ended I was quite unsure what I would learn from this. When I was asked what happened to me, I related simply what I had experienced. It wasn't until I spoke to some people in the tea break that I realized that there were two distinct groups in this one large gathering. There were the regulars who had experience and were discreet. They appeared grounded and clear in what they knew. Then there were others who seemed to come to live out some kind of fantasy. I was chatting to one of the women serving tea. Her name was Effie. I asked her about the people who'd spoken, or allegedly allowed spirits to speak through them: 'Did you really believe those words were coming from evolved spiritual teachers?'

I remember her big smile as it flashed at me for the first

time. She gave a little laugh as she answered me. 'Whether I believe or not, doesn't make it real, but what did you think, kid? If it makes you think, then it's worth considering.' She laughed again and poured tea for a woman beside me. 'Mer tea Margaret, another new comer.' Smiling to herself, she got on with her work, leaving me none the wiser. It seemed an enigmatic answer, but that's what these women seemed to be like. They lived in a world that frowned on Spiritualism and they had to protect what they believed in.

Despite my slight misgivings, I went along the following Thursday and thereafter for the next few months. After a while I began to understand a little about what was happening. I was making friends with the more serious-minded members, those with a more intellectual approach. We shared books and had discussion nights. I knew that some of the mediums and healers had emerged from this development group, but I couldn't work out how one went from attending the meetings to being able to give messages or heal people. Whenever I asked Mrs Primrose questions about the spirit world she would be just as enigmatic as Effie had been. 'It's the spirits in *this* world that you need to focus on first, son. Fix wits closest tae yae, then everything else will fall into place.' Then, she marched off towards the kitchen. 'Effie, huv yae goat a tea fur me?'

I had lots of things to fix at that time. Katie had fallen into her old ways, forgetting to pay bills and she was still just as quick to tell barefaced lies about it.

'Katie, why are all the lights not working, have you called anyone to fix them?' I asked one night after coming home from work.

'The power's off. Apparently workmen cut a cable when

they were digging the roads today.' The first time she said this it didn't dawn on me to check. Another time I tried to call my mother from our house and the line was dead. 'Do you know that they stupid workmen cut right through the phone lines when they were here this morning, I told them that we want a rebate on our next bill because of the inconvenience.' How much do we owe? is what I should have said. But for some reason I just gave her more money. I think I had lost the will to fight over it. It may have been that deep down there were stirrings of guilt about coming to believe I might be gay.

We were finding it hard to manage in all departments of our life together. The interest rates on our mortgage had risen to as high as fourteen and a half percent, which was more than double the rate it had started at. We just couldn't keep up the payments. I used to worry a lot about this kind of thing, but rather than shout about it I would internalize things and drive myself crazy. My mother would have loved to tell me that taking on a mortgage had been a big mistake: 'Ah told yae that a mortgage was the wrang thing tae dae. Did yae see the news? That bastard Thatcher is gonnay cripple this fucking country. I wish ah could get her in a room on my own fur five fucking minutes. Ah no wit ah wid dae wae her.' It wasn't any help, but I believed that was her attempt at being supportive. I should have passed on my mother's number to Arthur Scargill. If he'd had Lizzy on his side he might have had a better chance standing up to Maggie.

We sold our flat in Garthland Drive just two years after moving in and were astonished when we made a profit of more than ten thousand pounds. It was the most amazing thing. I talked to our solicitor who told me that we should buy something else, using some of the money as a deposit, but keep the rest to pay off debts. It all sounded brilliant, lifting some of the pressure out of our lives for a while. Get some money and that will sort out your life's problems. I imagine lots of people feel like that. But it really isn't the answer when you find that you have stopped communicating with your other half and you're both hiding things from each other. My life in the Spiritualist church was something which I didn't talk to Katie about. Whenever she asked me anything I would give vague answers which ended the conversation quickly.

I was no longer bothered by Katie's elaborate stories about debts or her justifications for spending. I was leading my own life. I was on a quest to learn everything I could about the occult, spiritualism and all things other-worldly. It was my own private world and I didn't want to open it up to anyone who wouldn't understand it. I only really talked to Katie if it was about the boys, their needs and wants, their school.

It wasn't long before I got a real urge to be free of my life as it was. I was twenty-seven and I felt that I was just starting to get to know myself. After a couple of years sitting in meditation groups, I was beginning to understand that the work I was doing in the development circle was allowing me to let go of my fear. The truth was beginning to bubble up. The group created a place of safety and support to encourage this. Self-analysis and deep soul-searching was helping me reach the real me, the person I had tried to keep from myself for most of my life.

But it wasn't easy because once you find yourself you have to face yourself. Then you have to take responsibility for your own actions . . .

I believed that I had outgrown my marriage. I hadn't

stopped loving Katie, but I just didn't know how to any more. I had no physical urges or need for sex at that time. I probably resented not having explored my life, a desire I had lost or had to put aside when I had become a parent so young. Neither had Katie had a chance to explore any other desires or aspirations. How can you when you fall in love, have a child and get married before you even begin to ask yourself serious questions about your own life?

Katie and I had been arguing a lot. Her mother had been living with us for years now, I was exhausted and money was still very tight. I realized that I couldn't go on with this. It wasn't because I knew I was gay – I was still not admitting this to myself – but because Katie wasn't willing to take the steps I wanted to. Katie only ever wanted us to go out and get drunk with her friends. She hated my attachment to the Spiritualist church, which I was going to more and more frequently. She said it was like a cult.

So one night when we'd gone out to a restaurant, I said I thought I didn't want to carry on with the marriage. Katie was very angry about this and said she wanted us to try to fix it, but I didn't. And I didn't want to argue.

It was the hardest thing I had ever done in my life, and I still feel an emotional wrench when I think of how I decided to leave my children. I moved out.

I reassured them I wasn't that far away and that I'd visit several nights a week and every weekend. I tried to remain as involved as I could. I love my sons and it was important for me that they knew I would always be there if they needed me.

It was very difficult for Katie too. I know she felt the same distance between us, but I think she thought the problems could just be hidden away under a drawer or papered over.

I had had enough of looking for lies, I wanted to search for truths instead, and when you put yourself out on a limb for such a thing, you can't just accept the usual, the ordinary. For me it was time to wake up a latent ability within me, to wake up and experience more than my limited life had afforded me. There was a force alive inside me and I wanted to see where it would lead. I trusted that there was a reason great enough to just try walking away from my normal life with a wife and two sons.

The next year of my life was the most difficult I can remember. Emotionally, I was drained and physically I was exhausted from trying to be in so many places in one day.

The new house we had bought was in Cumbernauld, a new town outside Glasgow where the houses were much cheaper than the city. Katie had friends and family who lived there and many people from the church lived there too. It was nice to have people around who we knew, but it was difficult to keep our business from them and we were trying to do that with most people then.

I was now spending the majority of my time in Sammy's council flat in the city. He'd moved in with a new woman, but dad had insisted that he didn't let the flat go, knowing Sammy's record. So at least I could live there for free.

For all the changes the boys carried on as normal. They went off to school, brought their friends back to the house and played on their new computer game – God, the world was changing. We were separated but tried not to let it upset our sons' world too much. When Katie wanted to go out with friends I would watch the boys. They didn't seem to ask many questions at first. I'm not sure if that was because I didn't want them to or if they were just too busy being young boys. But eventually they began to work it out and it broke my heart when Steven asked me why I had to go and when would I be back. I wasn't ready to answer him then. I don't suppose I *had* the answers, I was still trying to work them out myself. There was really only one person I could talk to openly about my feelings.

Jim McManus was my closest friend at that time. He had not long split with his girlfriend and had recently lost his father. He was going through his own emotional stuff. He was there for me to talk to and he also allowed me to just be quiet and reflective if I needed that more.

We first met at a meditation night in the Spiritualist church, when he came along with one of the regulars. I didn't particularly notice him at first, perhaps because he wasn't deeply into all the spiritualist stuff himself, being a Catholic. He was more interested in learning how to meditate, and so he was spending time with our other group. But when he found out that we did healing nights at the church, my friends in the meditation group told me about him and said they thought he had a healing temperament. After that he started to attend the church more. Jim had seen healing of sorts with a new charismatic group his mother was part of within the Catholic church, so he became interested in the healing we did. It was clear to me that his life was going through changes like mine, and we had a natural empathy.

Jim was living in Cumbernauld near Katie and the boys. He'd had to sell his little flat when he left his job to help care for his father. I told Jim about my brother Sammy's flat and that I was using it when I stayed in town. If he wanted, I said, he could have the second bedroom until he got things sorted. This suited him. He didn't want to commit to a lease or anything because he planned to go off round Europe for a while and just find himself. As I said, we could relate to one another, because we were both in very similar places and also, neither really got in the other's way.

What with going from work to the boys at night, staying in Sammy's flat in the Gorbals and still attending the development circle, I found that my head was dizzy by the end of an evening. I was avoiding visiting my parents – something you do when you don't want a lecture from Lizzy. My mother and father always had an uncanny ability to know everything that was going on with me, even when there was no way they could know. I learned that ability can come with parenthood. I wasn't surprised then, when I eventually called my mother, that the first words out of her mouth were, 'Huv you and Katie split up? See, ah told yur da, they've split up. Where ur you living? Ar you using oor Sammy's flat? Don't go spending money yae huvney goat . . .' I hated that she knew, and I felt invaded that she was talking about things that weren't her business.

It's a weird phenomenon I've noticed over the years with people who are on a spiritual journey; at some point they seem to have to go through what's sometimes called 'the dark night of the soul'. It's a critical point on the path when you are rendered helpless by the events of your life. It all becomes too much to grapple with and circumstances seem beyond your control. You reach the point of not caring if you live or die. Some people who hit this state of helplessness have nothing to hold onto and drop into deep depressions, losing faith and hope. But if you trust in something bigger than you, a force behind everything that will help you, come what may, then as you freefall through the abyss of your mind beyond all emotions, something happens.

I went through this almost dying myself. I just didn't know who I was, or what I was. But all the while I had a deep feeling that there was an intelligent spiritual mind that was somewhere close. I believed I should trust in the invisible guidance I sensed. Believing this means that you are either gullible and weak, or brave enough to follow your conviction.

Mrs Primrose had proved to be a strong leader in the development circle – strident if necessary but compassionate when required. She had advised me to have healing. She told me about a man she just called John. A very fatherly figure, he gave me healing every week, bringing a calm to my mind and body like I'd never felt before. It was John's work that really changed everything for me. He would simply place his hands on my shoulders. It felt almost like a sedative. I wouldn't be able to think any more and then I'd drift off somewhere. Then I'd be aware of his hands again. He never spoke except to say, 'Ar ye alright, son?' After his healing I would feel balance. After six weeks of his healing he had cleared me of fear.

I was also being trained in spiritual healing by Effie, the tea lady I had met that first night at the circle, and who became my great friend. Effie was one of the most down to earth teachers I ever encountered during my development. She just kept things real. When you are freefalling, you need someone who is in touch with the ground.

After I had been to the circle for five years, I had learned quite a bit about who I really was. Even if I didn't totally understand everything about my life, at least I now felt awake and I could see the world in a very different way. I realized that the mediumship was something I had been born with. It didn't need developing. It was me who needed developing. I needed to be truthful and self-aware and then the gift of mediumship I was born with could come into its own. That was the most important thing I had learned about mediumship to that point. Then suddenly my gift was put on display in front of a packed church.

Mrs Primrose, our regular medium, was at another Spiritualist meeting in Glasgow. We were supposed to have a lady visiting in her stead, but she didn't show. We didn't have anybody to take her place it seemed. Usually in this situation, there would be a medium in the congregation who would step up, but not tonight. That left three of us in Mrs Primrose's office wondering what we were going to tell the packed congregation.

'Stevie, why don't you give a talk on mediumship, they might like that?' Mima, the church secretary, asked our vice president. I was with them in the office because I was going to give a poetry reading, a regular part of the service on a Tuesday night. I was quiet and didn't get involved in the discussion while I tried to practise the piece I'd chosen. But something in my gut told me that I would be doing the mediumship. On the way to church in the car I had actually heard a voice telling me to get ready. This was unusual. I was startled and filled up with feelings of nervous anticipation. At the time, I had no idea what I was to get ready for, but now I did. I let the other two argue the point for another five minutes. We were running late. Then Stevie looked at me and said, 'Gordon, will you do it? You can do it, I just know you can.'

'That's a great idea,' Mima agreed. 'You always give people

good messages when you're healing them in the healing class.' Did I? Whether I did or didn't I wasn't prepared for this. But then I realized that I no longer felt sick and anxious. Hearing the voice earlier in the car had given me time to get over my nerves and I felt clear.

'Just trust spirit,' Mima said as she looked at me, pleadingly. She was the booking secretary and people would have looked to her if no medium turned up on a service night.

'Ok, I'll try it. But I have no idea what I'm doing and they will just have to accept this.' We went into the hall, and I walked to the front through the narrow gap between the chairs. That night, there wasn't a single empty one.

My first attempt at mediumship felt completely spontaneous. In that very moment I think I prayed to every God, idol and deity under the sun for help. If I believed I was a medium and I *really* trusted spirit as a force, then this was the moment when either my trust was rewarded or I would be left looking like a twat in front of a crowded room. I gave out a last silent prayer, 'Please God, I promise I'll stop smoking if yae make this work.' There, that ought to do it.

I don't remember much of what happened or what I said, but I know that the moment I stood up, I was filled with the same calm I had felt when John healed me. I felt that there was a force controlling every word that came through my mouth. I didn't speak in another voice like some of the people in the development circle, but I was confident in an amazing energy which was beyond anything I'd ever experienced. There was no doubt about the messages that came through. To be honest, people were speechless when it was over. The minute I'd finished, my nerves returned and I started to shake like a leaf while Stevie read the notices for the coming week.

'Wow, were did that come from?' When we got back to the office, Mima grabbed me and gave me a big hug.

'That wasn't me, Mima. It was spirit or something. But wow, you're right. I don't know what happened there.'

'That *was* spirit. I could feel the change when I was sitting behind you, Gordon.' Stevie spoke calmly to me and with certainty. 'Wait till Mrs P hears about this!' Crap, I hadn't thought about this. She would probably never have let me go on the platform. My development wasn't finished. Besides, she had told me to develop in healing, not mediumship. I could imagine her reprimanding me when she walked into the church later that night. I thought about getting out before she came back, but I didn't, I would just brave it out.

I didn't have to worry. After she stared into my eyes for a moment and pondered on what Stevie had just told her, she softened. 'Ok, it was always going tae happen, it's just sooner than I thought. But from now on, I will take you personally on the platform with me until you learn how to do this right. Is that understood?' It was, and I was relieved she'd implied that she'd always knew I would be a medium. I came to learn that Mrs Primrose knew many things she didn't talk about until she had to.

But oh my God, I was to be an actual medium! Just as Mary Duffy had predicted and also that woman Sadie my parents had taken me to see when I was young.

Everyone in the church was very touched by the way I had given messages that night. There were plenty of questions: 'How did you get that woman's husband's name like that? Did yae hear it, Gordon?' Or, 'When you told that woman she lived in Preston Street, where did that come from?' All the people I sat in the circle with were talking about what I'd just done and there was a real buzz. The only thing was, I had no idea how it worked. If I'm honest, I couldn't remember a word I'd spoken. It was great to be told I was a medium, but it wasn't as though I'd passed an exam or learned any techniques. It was just in me.

After that night my life as a medium began. I shared the platform with my mentor a few times before she decided that I was ready to go out to the other Spiritualist churches in the area and demonstrate my gift. One of those churches would be Somerset Place, where I had been told five years earlier that I would be standing on that very platform doing what Mary Duffy had done.

Mediumship was only one part of the spiritual side of my life. I now understood that my experience in develop-ment was about finding the spirit in me, as well as becoming more self-aware. And so now my life was turning a corner. In the dark emotionally confused maze my life had been, I was now finding a path that was becoming clearer and more defined. I can see now that this was something I had to own. The potential to be a medium had always been there and it was my choice whether to follow that path, or not.

Everyone has something latent in them, something which could be ignited in their life, but there are responsibilities that come with it. But if you're sincere and give yourself wholeheartedly to your gift, the cost isn't so great.

If you are hiding secrets in your life, it's hard to be sincere in anything that means a lot to you. My develop-ment group helped me to get rid of the fear attached to those secrets. If you meditate regularly and go into a silent state of self, eventually you will meet the real you and that is what happened to me around this time. I realized that since I was young I'd been gay. Just like the mediumship, it was there lying dormant, I suppose. When you start to clear out the cupboards of your mind you will find things at the back that you always said you would deal with and didn't.

Jim and I found ourselves in a place and time where we just couldn't ignore the obvious any more. We were living together and had very strong feelings for each other. Jim was quiet and calm – very different to my family. His mother had wanted him to be a priest and he'd trained for the priesthood, then he'd worked as a nurse and a care-worker. He had a naturally caring nature. I was to learn, too, that he was a born healer, a gift he developed when he took a course at Mrs Primrose's church. So he had a spiritual view of life, he was someone I could talk to, and on top of all that he played the guitar and I liked to sing.

I knew he had recently broken up with a long term girlfriend and then I found out that he'd also had a gay relationship which had turned out badly. There was freedom in all of this I'd never experienced before, though of course I didn't tell Lizzy and my dad, my brothers or Katie. We both knew that there was a bond of love between us, and that it was growing. It was such a confusing, frightening time I remember, but as with the mediumship, I think that sometimes when we are afraid, we just have to take a chance.

Between us we had endured years of sexual repression. Even if a person from our neck of the woods knew they were homosexual, they could never be open about it. There was a stigma attached to it. Once again, I look back and think how much easier this would have been if we all had the courage to talk openly about our feelings.

***

Two people arrived in my life around this time. The first was a practitioner of Tibetan Buddhism, someone whose niece happened to be going out with my brother, Sammy. His girlfriend's name was Dee and she was lovely, a really nice person. Mother also liked Dee. In fact everyone did, she just had a friendly air about her. She told me that I should meet her aunt who she said was into some of the things I was. I was intrigued and when she offered to take me to meet her the following Sunday, I accepted. Her aunt lived in the countryside near Stirling, so I thought it would be great to take the boys for a day out.

Dee and I chatted the whole journey about life, relationships, broken relationships, new relationships and it was clear that, even though she didn't know me, she kind of got me. I liked Dee, but with her aunt it was a whole other level, not just because of the Buddhism. She was quite amazingly attuned to everything I spoke about – and I suppose I was the same with her. It was obvious to me within a second of meeting her, that she was a natural psychic, but more than that, she was just a woman who knew things.

Her Buddhist name was Dronma and that is how I always refer to her. She is a very successful artist, living in a village in the mountains, which some days sits above the clouds.

My sons loved her place. Within only five minutes of being introduced to her she whipped on a coat and assumed we all knew we were going out. We followed her as she briskly made her way up country lanes and into fields, all the while giving the boys a lesson in botany. Soon they knew that certain plants could be eaten while others had qualities to heal or colour things. Dronma was a real force of nature whose conversation changed from one thing to the next. Yet each thing she spoke about involved a question that one of us had thought of, but hadn't yet asked. I wondered if all Buddhists were like this and as soon as I'd had the thought she said, 'You know, Buddhists are normally quiet and meditative. I suppose I'm more noisy than most.' Either this lady was a natural telepath, or the place we were in was between two worlds or something. My son Paul even said, 'Dronma, this place is like middle earth isn't it?' The kids were reading the ether around her too.

Later Dee and the boys fell asleep in front of her open log fire which smelled of pine cones and peat. It was then that Dronma and I spoke properly to one another. I learned that she was on her own spiritual path, but was going through relationship problems. Before we knew it, we were finishing each other's sentences. I don't know why, but Dee's aunt made me feel that my spiritual path was right and that no matter how many people criticized what I was doing, not using my gift would be worse. I believe I was able to help shift things for her too.

Then as I was leaving she came out to the car, leaned in the window and said something that gave me the courage to move to the next level of my relationship with Jim: 'Gordon, I know we spoke at each other a lot and it seems like we both have stuff to deal with, but you have something that troubles you on a relationship level that we haven't touched on. I can just feel it. I might not be able to fix it for you, but I get a sense that it will be ok if you just go with it. Sometimes it's what we're supposed to do.' Wow, it was the answer I wanted to hear and it came from a stranger.

The other person who appeared on the scene was Tom Barker. La Barker, as I call him now, was the brother of Frances who had been murdered. Like my meeting with Dee's aunt, bumping into Tom came at the perfect time. Having finally started a sexual relationship with my best friend, I was going around like a fart in a trance, worrying about what the world would think of me. I was walking down Buchanan Street in Glasgow when I heard a familiar voice calling out. The voice was clear and strong and it halted me in my tracks: 'Excuse me, excuse me.' I turned slightly and saw, moving towards me, a very well-dressed, slim man with a shock of blonde curls on top of his head. 'Aren't you cousin Liz's boy? Sammy isn't it?' I smiled because I knew straight away that this was Tom. Lizzy had always said I should meet him.

I had only ever seen him once before a long time ago. He arrived at Mansel Street in an open-topped Lancia and stayed for about thirty seconds to say hello to my mother. She always insisted he wasn't gay for some reason. 'Oh naw, oor Tom isnay a queer, he jest talks nice, that awe.'

Of all people to meet when I was going through my crisis! Considering I had walked down this street hundreds of times in my life before this, it was very fortuitous to run into him right now.

'Gordon, Tommy. I'm Gordon.'

'Oh Gordon, you are the youngest one, that's right. But do call me Tom.' He was definite about his pronunciation, but it sounded more like Dom. 'How interesting I should meet you because one of my close friends was just talking about you. Now you are the hairdresser, is that right?' Such was my paranoia, I thought he was going to say he knew I was gay. 'Now, is it true you live in Cumbernauld?'

'Er, yes.'

'Ok, now would it be possible for you to cut my hair? I find that I'm between hairdressers and I heard that you are a good cutter. I only live five minutes from you.' He didn't mention gay once. I was relieved: 'Sure Dom, eh, Tommy, eh.'

He produced a black pen with a shiny gold lid from his top pocket, wrote his phone number on a small piece of paper and handed it to me: 'You were right the first time darling, it's Dom. Call me later and we'll sort out an appointment for my hair.' He spun on his heels like a dancer and sort of glided along the street in the other direction. People were looking at him, but he didn't notice them, or maybe he did and this was the effect he wanted. He disappeared into a crowd of passers-by all stopping to look at the phenomenon that was Dom.

Meeting Tom in his home was very different from meeting him in the street. He was tougher, more like the other Barkers that I had met, Aunt Annie and Frances and his sister Margaret who lived in the flats next to my parents. He introduced me to his partner Robert, whom Tom referred to as Dada. The flat they lived in looked swish like no other flat I had ever seen, glamorous with crystal chandeliers, leather sofas and heavy velvet drapes. It didn't look gay at all . . .

I would go to cut Tom's hair regularly after our first appointment and we laughed so much when he told stories about his life.

'Would you say you were a half-glass-full kind of person, or a half-glass-empty?' I asked him once.

After a moment's consideration he came back with, 'Well, that all depends on whose face I was throwing it over, darling.' He then erupted into a great big guffaw and his hands opened almost expecting applause. He always made me laugh when he told me how he'd dealt with people who picked on him for being gay. Tom wasn't just out, in his words. 'There is out, and then there is fifty miles of fabulous and then there's La Barker.' His camp humour was, of course, his defence. A very coarse woman once asked him, 'So you're a poof, wits that like then?' Tom didn't get ruffled. Instead, he drew himself up to his full height, looked her straight in the eye and smiled before saying, 'Well my dear, why don't you ask your husband, I was with him the whole of last night.' Spin on heels, sharp exit. The woman was left with her bottom jaw on the floor.

But Tom's life wasn't all sarcasm, quips and witty gay banter. He was beaten up many times. He told me that the police in Glasgow were the worst offenders, but he never changed his behaviour no matter what. I think for me it was good to hear how Tom came through his life as a gay man in Glasgow. He taught me never to be ashamed of who I am, and that people who had problems with homosexuals usually had hidden desires they were ashamed of. In such cases we were just mirrors for these people. Robert and Tom were very nurturing to me and I will never forget them for this. They helped me see beyond the prejudice and ignorance that people had towards homosexuality and to grow more as a person in the process.

I think certain people come into your life when you are ready to meet them. Life may be hard at times, but it is made much easier when you have people around you who are themselves no matter what. These are people who have gone beyond criticism or judgment, people who are themselves because they love and trust who they are. I had found two people who were very different from one another, yet who both believed in being totally honest about who they were. Dronma and the fabulous La Barker taught me a valuable lesson: 'Go do it anyway.'

13

Living In Two Worlds

Who knew? I was a twenty-nine-year old hairdresser, father of two, with an ex-wife and a gay partner and I spoke to dead people. Who doesn't know someone like that? By this time Christine had left hairdressing to train as a social worker and I now worked on a percentage with Katie's Uncle John at City Barbers, a busy salon in town. The more you cut, the more you earned. I remember a guy in his early twenties asking me if I gave a consultation before I began the cut. He said his usual stylist did this and he looked at me in the mirror, expectantly. I asked where he normally got his hair cut and how much he usually paid.

'I've been going to Irvin Rusk. It costs about thirty quid. Why?'

'Ok,' I told him. 'We charge a fiver and here is the consultation. Would you like a number one, two, three, or four up the back and sides, and how much off the top?' That's how we rolled in City Barbers.

As a father of two I was still juggling all my commitments with my priority being to spend time with the boys. I continued to drive over as many week nights after work as I could. I kept up the weekend visits too. So I'd have them on Saturday after work and bring them back on Sunday nights.

The boys were ten and seven and it still didn't feel like the right time to tell them about Jim. They knew him and liked him and when they stayed over at weekends and on holidays it was obvious we lived together.

Paul was doing well at school, gaining all sorts of awards and accolades for his work. It was easy to be proud of him. Steven was also very bright and got good grades. He was more sporty and loved playing football and tennis or going swimming. (He became quite good at tennis, though he never managed to beat me at it. It's my story Steven, so when you write your book you can change the tennis score.)

After the first year or so following the split up with Katie, my raw emotional state was beginning to settle. Though it was costing as much money as I was making to run two homes, it meant that the boys could still have some sense of normality where possible.

Katie and I were just about on speaking terms. She wanted me to tell her more about what was happening in my life, but I found that hard at the time. I was trying to get used to it myself and if I'm honest I still ran a mile from anyone who tried to question me about what I was doing.

Life became more difficult for Katie when her old Grandad Joe passed away. It was a very sad loss for all the family because he was the centre of that world and such a big character. Paul took it as badly as his mother. I think it was the first time I ever saw him lose his temper. He snapped at me from the back seat of the car when I drove him home that Sunday evening. I remember how much it hurt.

Sammy's relationship with his new woman came to an end around this time, so he needed the flat back. Jim and I had moved from my brother's flat to the worst place in the world. It seemed as though all the neighbours were junkies and there were often stabbings. Every night we watched police cars and ambulances pull up to the flats. More often than not they left with blue lights flashing and sirens blasting out. I remember I wanted so much to be somewhere that was quiet. On a bad day, I would wonder if being in this place was like a penance or some kind of karmic retribution for being gay.

One morning just before waking I had this dream that I was talking to an older man and Mary Duffy, the medium I had seen for the first time with Christine. The three of us were standing in a park. I recognized it as the Glasgow Green not far from where my parents lived. In the dream there was a funfair on the Green, as there was every July. The man was pointing in a westerly direction and as I looked I saw the Spiritualist church in Berkeley Street where I'd received the great message from Ummy. Finally, Mrs Duffy spoke to me: 'This will bring you peace of mind, son.' Then I woke but the dream would not leave my mind. I told Jim about it, thinking it would go away, but it didn't.

Later that evening I was working in one of the small churches in Glasgow. Terri, a booking secretary from the Berkeley Street church, asked me if I'd be free to serve her church on Sunday of that week. Mary Duffy was sick and had had to cancel. 'How funny,' I said, and told her about having a dream about Mary that morning. And I agreed to serve the church that weekend.

I had never worked on that particular platform before. When I finished I was taken downstairs for a cup of tea to a flat in the basement I didn't know existed. Terri began asking me about future dates. She also told me they needed a caretaker to live in the flat and look after the church. They didn't think it would be easy to find anyone, she said, because people would think there might be spirits hanging around. We both just laughed and then I had a thought: Jim was looking for a little part time job and if he became the live-in caretaker, our horrible existence in the east end flat from hell would be over. I mentioned this to Terri and she said she would ask the committee when they had their next meeting.

Just as I was leaving the church another of the church secretaries stopped me and asked if I would consider being part of a big event in Somerset Place to celebrate the church's 100th anniversary. She said I would be working with Mary Duffy and Albert Best, one of the most renowned mediums in the world. Anyone who was interested in Spiritualism or mediumship would have heard of Mr Best then. I said yes without hesitation. I really respected Mary as a medium, but this man really was the best. His name had come up on that very first visit to the Spiritualist church with Christine. Mary Duffy had suggested we contact him, but it turned out he was away in India. He spent a lot of time abroad. Mrs Duffy said she felt sure that Brian would come through Albert for Christine if we contacted him. Christine had moved on by now, but I had seen Albert twice at the Berkeley Street church and been amazed by his accuracy. He was the most evidential medium I had ever seen. He was the uncle of George Best and had the same aura of magic about him and the same startling green eyes. He *had* given me a message from Brian as Mrs Duffy had predicted, and asked that we meet after the service, but I'd had to rush off to pick up the kids.

Over the past couple of years I had spent more and more time travelling round Glasgow, then Scotland, serving a number of Spiritualist churches. Many people were becoming interested in my mediumship. I was getting a lot of requests to do evenings to raise money for charity and such. I had no idea what people thought about me or what I was doing as a medium, because I had too many things going on in my life to get caught up with stuff like that. But to be asked to work on the same platform as Mary and Albert was something that did make me take note. This told me that the Spiritualist world was taking me seriously.

I was worried about working with these two great mediums. Just as I was sharing my anxiety with Jim, our phone rang. It was Terri. She said that Jim had got the job as caretaker, that we could have the flat and we could move in just two weeks from now. That would be the middle of July during the fortnight of the Glasgow Fair. Then it dawned on me that in my dream, I'd seen Mary and the elderly man, who I now realized was Albert Best. I remembered that in the dream they'd been on Glasgow Green, and he'd been pointing towards the church in Berkeley Street. It all fitted. We were to be free from the horrible, dark place we were living in and were moving into the centre of Glasgow, where it would be peaceful, as I heard Mary say in the dream.

Our new home was amazing. A nice, big, Georgian high-ceilinged flat, it was quiet and we had no neighbours. I honestly think for the first time in my life I found some true peace of mind.

That is, until I had to go and do the special night with Albert Best. Mrs Duffy couldn't manage to get to Glasgow that night, as she was poorly. However, the church was happy they had Albert and me to demonstrate to their two hundred and fifty guests. I have since stood and worked as a medium to crowds as big as five thousand in Australia and America, but I've never been more nervous than I was to work along-side a little Irishman from Belfast.

I remember him looking right at me and asking, 'Do you really hear spirits, son?' I didn't know how to answer him, and just looked at him. He wasn't joking either. Did he think I was making this up? My legs shook the way they had the first night at Mrs Primrose's, but this was different. I not only had to prove my truth to the audience, but to someone who was a legend in his field.

That evening was one of those moments in my life when I don't recall exactly what I said, but whatever it was worked. A medium knows when they have a good connection to the other side. The evidence that comes through from the spirit world becomes very exact. We never ask questions when we are in such a flow, we only give exact statements.

Mr Best liked what I did. At the end of my session he announced he was excited to work with a true young medium. He said that he was happy, that he saw in me great potential to take my gift around the world, and he said I would help many people.

This was the greatest honour any medium could have gotten from someone like Albert. He was the kind of man to tell the truth and if he thought someone was a fake or just deluded, he would also tell them. As far as talking to the dead goes, it was the best endorsement any young medium could have been given. Not only did he like my work, but also we became friends for the rest of his life. I think he told everyone he ever worked with about me and encouraged them to invite me to demonstrate for them. I am proud that Albert Best believed in me. It meant more than anything to me as a medium and even today I can still genuinely feel his essence when I remember his words: 'Gordon, help people with your gift. That's what it's really for.'

I didn't know it at the time, but it was Albert Best who suggested to Professor Archie Roy of Glasgow University that he observe my mediumship. Professor Archie Roy was Emeritus Professor of Astronomy at the university. He was interested in testing what was said by a medium. Sometimes he would observe public demonstrations, but he also conducted rigorous scientific trials at the university alongside Tricia Robertson, a statistician. This had started out as a private project, but the results were so significant that Professor Roy went on to publish three papers on it. The trials involved double-blind tests to ensure against bias on either side. My score was 98 per cent accuracy. I'm told this is the highest of any of the mediums tested.

In the next couple of years Jim would see his mother pass to the spirit world. We both grew very fond of Albert before he too passed over. My old teacher Mrs Primrose, graciously went to sleep one night and woke up on the other side. But death didn't have the same sting for me as it might have done. I realized that death isn't always the worst thing to touch our lives when we are in this physical world. Sometimes it's tougher to watch a loved one suffer than to let them go.

Around this time, I met an elderly gentleman called Gordon Gunn. He came to see me one day for a private reading in the church at Berkeley Street. I had never met this man before in my life and had no idea of his loss. However, two minutes into the reading his good lady wife came through from the spirit world and gave him the biggest telling-off I ever remember witnessing in my work as a medium. She told me to tell him she was furious with him because he was thinking about suicide, as he was lonely without her. At the end of the session he admitted that he had pills at home which he had been considering taking and that if he had not gotten any message from his wife that day, he would have gone ahead. He was blown away that his wife knew all about these things. Soon I think he understood what I already knew, that we can't die. We can't die for the life of us. His wife had come through to him because his grief was such that it had been eating at him like some slow cancer. The man had been in a living hell until his dear wife came through like a burst of lightning and snapped him out of it. I was glad.

Gordon and I became great friends despite the age gap and he helped me to open a new salon in Glasgow called Gentry. Gordon was retired, but he loved the idea that Jim and I might open our own salon together (Jim was also now trained as a gent's barber). He encouraged us and lent us the start up costs.

Gordon was sometimes annoyed at me because I never took money when I did readings. He was a great businessman, a real asset to have in your corner when you start out on your own business. Before long our salon in the west end of Glasgow was buzzing. We had the idea of doing old-fashioned hot towel shaves and gent's facials, as well as haircuts. The salon looked olde-worlde and this attracted lots of attention from magazines and newspapers wanting to do photo shoots.

I tried to do as much demonstrating of my mediumship as I could, despite being very busy at the salon, and I took it all very seriously. One particular night, I set off to visit a church some twenty miles outside Glasgow. I'd arranged to meet Chrissie, the church President, at the Motherwell turn off. But I ended up getting lost, and by the time I arrived she'd gone, probably assuming I wasn't coming. I hadn't got the exact address of the venue, and now I was running late. Then I had a brainwave. The meeting was being held in the local Scout hall. I asked a passer-by for directions to the local police station, thinking they'd be able to tell me where it was.

It was a very wet night. Once I'd parked outside the police station I ran from the car through the torrential rain and burst in through the doors to reception. Out of breath, and dripping wet, I stood there in my long raincoat panting and asked the desk sergeant if he could please direct me to the local Scout hall. He gave me a look that suggested he was weighing up whether or not I was some kind of crazy pervert. So taking a deep breath I told him that I was a medium and explained my situation. Of course, it wasn't the first time someone had made a crack along the lines of: if you're a medium then surely the spirits will guide you, but eventually he gave me directions and off I went.

I found the hall easily and looking through the glass doors into the room I could see quite a large crowd gathered inside. It looked like I was in luck and they hadn't started yet. My heart was still pumping hard from rushing to get there, as I hurried into the hall apologizing profusely for being late. The congregation looked somewhat surprised to see me and a man standing on a raised platform in front of them asked me who I was and why I was here. 'I'm Gordon Smith,' I replied, perplexed. 'I'm the medium.' As my eyes scanned the room, it was only then that I had a horrible realization. There out of the corner of my eye I could now see a large poster which read: 'Jesus Saves All Sinners'. I wasn't supposed to be here. This was a born-again Christian meeting. I was in the wrong Scout hall! I didn't hang around. I legged it back to the car before I could be pounced on and led off to be exorcised.

When I got home I called Chrissie who, far from sympathizing, laughed hysterically.

One day in Gentry I was cutting a man's hair. Suddenly I felt my mind being pulled into a kind of daydream, but one which felt like it was real. I was in an office and my mother was there too with my dad and my brother Jonny. I almost fainted when I heard the voice of the doctor telling my mother that she had throat cancer. Coming to, I ran into the back of the shop and searched for my mobile phone. I called Lizzy's home number but there was no answer, so I switched to my brother's mobile number and it just rang out. I told Jim what I had just experienced. He knew me well enough to know that I didn't make this stuff up, that I was as grounded as it gets, especially when it comes to family.

'Have you been worried about your mum, or has she said anything?'

'No, it just happened and it was real. I didn't just see it, I actually felt it too.'

Seeing things in your imagination is one thing, but when you feel the happening like it's inside you, . . . well, this told me that what I was seeing almost certainly wasn't mere imagination. Those feelings running through me were also running through my mother. I just had to get it confirmed. When I knew for certain, I would get a sense of what to do next.

Ten minutes later I got an answer to Lizzy's house phone. It was Jonny who answered. 'Jonny, has ma ma got cancer?'

There was a silence at the other end before my brother confirmed what I already knew. He and my parents had just arrived back at the flat from the doctor's and hadn't made a single call to anyone. I told him that I was coming over to be with my parents but he wisely told me to wait for a bit. He said that the whole family would be there and maybe it would be better for me to wait till everyone had gone, then come over and talk to her on my own. I agreed, but my insides were constantly churning as my mind asked questions of the spirit world. What to do best for my mother?

No answers came back to me. I didn't expect them to. There are certain times in this life when we can't get help and sadly this was one of them. My mother was a fighter, she was tough and my father was wise. He would be the best and most comforting person she could have beside her.

It is a horrible thing when one of your parents becomes ill. They give you everything they have and work for you, feed and clothe you and above all else, love you in their own unique way. Then at a moment like this when you should be rushing to them with answers and solutions and hope, you are rendered helpless.

My mother's condition was at a stage when there was treatment available, an operation to remove her larynx. But it would have to be done within days rather than weeks. It was a lot to think about. Lizzy without a voice! On my way to visit her that evening I met Dronma. She had got news that same day that a family friend had a cancerous growth in her stomach. She was in much the same place I was, trying to work out how to approach this, how best to support or advise.

Dronma wondered if it might help my mother to hear that her friend, who was only in her twenties, had this awful illness and was also at the stage of deciding whether or not to have an operation. Who knows what's right or wrong, but when we arrived at my parents my mother looked like she was still in shock from the news she had received earlier. She was sitting on the edge of her chair. She looked so small and scared, something I don't ever recall my mother being in my entire life.

This was awful, I hated to see her like this. The strongest person I'd ever known in my life had retracted into herself. It was only when Dronma told her about her daughter that my mother showed any sign of hearing us. I think she genuinely felt for the girl and because Dronma actually spoke the word cancer, which most of my family were avoiding, it jolted my mother and made her listen.

Then I spoke to her about what I felt. I told my mother whatever she decided to do, everyone who loved her would be right beside her. Then the next words came out of my mouth spontaneously. 'Ma, you are a very strong woman and if you want to beat this I know you will find a way. I hope that you can just see this cancer as someone who is threatening the happiness of your family and will try to hurt us. I'm sure if you look at it like this you will find the strength to fight it. It's just another fight, and I've never seen you back down from a fight and Ma, I've never seen you lose one either.'

Something shifted in my mother's position in that moment and I knew she was reviewing the situation inside her mind. She sat up straight for the first time and took a deep breath. 'Fuck it,' she said. 'You're right. I'm damned if this bastard will beat me.' She looked around the room and she was

Lizzy again. 'Sammy, I'm getting the operation, and you,' she pointed at Dronma, 'Tell yur daughter tae dae the same. Fuck cancer.'

My mother had her larynx removed days later. The doctors said that they had removed all the cancer in that one operation.

I don't think any of our family ever thought that the cutting of her body would have been so extensive. I remember when I visited on the evening after the op my mouth fell open. As I looked at all my brothers and sisters, I knew they felt the same. My mother's neck was stapled from just under her left ear across her throat and down to the top of her chest. I think we all wanted to cry then and there. Lizzy looked completely washed out. It didn't feel right to have so many people around her and no one daring to say anything, so we all just stood staring at our mother with looks of horror and sympathy all over our faces.

Lizzy was conscious, but with wires and tubes connecting her to medical equipment, and, of course, what we weren't really prepared for – no voice. It was a very heavy atmosphere to say the least. It was as though we just realized that our champion had been battered and knocked about a bit. But her first reaction in front of all her family told us she'd truly won another fight. There was a little notepad and pencil the nurse had left beside the bed just before she allowed the family to come in. She'd told my mother that if she needed to communicate, she could write things down. It was just as the silent tension around my mother's bed had reached an unbearable pitch that she decided to grab the notepad and pencil. Betty jumped to help, as did Joan, but she shot them a feisty glance that said to leave her alone. We all stepped back. She made such a quick movement with her head that we all looked intensely in her direction and watched her scribble something on the little pad. She flashed the pad around at us. On first glance we saw a large smiley face and on closer inspection the words beneath: 'Cheer up, or fuck off.' Lizzy smiled broadly like she wanted to laugh. Moved and tearful, we all laughed and cried and hugged each other. She was truly ok.

A few weeks after the operation, a plastic speech valve was fitted that would make it possible for Lizzy to speak. It was interesting that when she swore her voice got stronger! We just put that down to good muscle memory.

Her voice changed with the valve. It was raspy and breathy, but it still sounded like Lizzy. When she learned to speak better through the valve I remember her saying, 'Gordon, I've decided, I'm gonnay LIVE till ah die.' These were the same words her brother Barney had said when he had been first diagnosed with lung cancer years earlier. It was like a family motto, maybe the cry of all Glasgow diehards.

It was a difficult time. My father was now almost crippled with rheumatoid arthritis, plus his hearing was starting to go. When you visited them at home, Lizzy would be straining the new voice valve trying to get him to hear her and poor dad would be struggling to make her out. Lizzy would push her finger roughly into the valve trying to get more sound out of it. 'Sammy, ya deaf wee bastard, ur yae fucking listening tae me?'

'Gordon, ah canny hear wit that wumin's saying, except for swearing, that's awe ah hear coming from that valve.'

'Gordon, listen tae me, he talks shite, ah know he can hear me he jest fucking pretends he disney. Awe his sisters were the same, fucking ignorant . . .'

This kind of exchange would make me feel better before I had to travel off somewhere. This was becoming more and more common. I had just finished making a documentary for the BBC called, *Mediums Talking to the Dead*. It was getting lots of good attention, even from many sceptics. Also, I had just been offered a book deal by Hay House Publishers to write three books on the subject of mediumship and the afterlife, which meant I would be travelling even more promoting them. So to say my life had changed was probably an understatement. I had no idea where this path was going to take me and could never have dreamed that I was about to travel the world and meet some wonderful people and experience stuff beyond my wildest dreams.

Talking about dreams, I had the most profound dream ten years before my mother died. I was flying from London to Glasgow. I had just met some TV producers who wanted me to make a series about mediums for television. I think I must have been exhausted or something because for some reason I dreamt I was on a flight from Zurich. This was a place I had never been to, so that was the first thing about this dream that was odd. Why Zurich? The other thing was that in the dream I was on my way to talk at my mother's funeral. In reality I'd spoken to her just before boarding the short flight from London only an hour earlier, so that was the second odd thing. Who knows what dreams are? Was this a dream a premonition or just my worst fears popping up to the surface to let me know they were still there?

As the wheels hit the runway in Glasgow that night the dream, or whatever it was, didn't belong in that moment. I woke up with a start. I was in my early forties now. There was such promise waiting to be realized and the sense of

Acknowledgements

Thanks for Mark Booth and all at Coronet and Hodder & Stoughton.